Brigitte et Gilles Delluc, Alain Roussot, Julia Roussot-Larroque

DISCOVERING PÉRIGORD PREHISTORY

Alain Roussot, editor

Translated by Stanley L. OLIVIER

Brigitte and Gilles DELLUC,
Doctors in Prehistory, U.A. 184 of the C.N.R.S. and Abri Pataud, Les Eyzies.

Alain ROUSSOT,
Conservator at the Musée d'Aquitaine and U.A. 880 of the C.N.R.S.

Julia ROUSSOT-LARROQUE,
Director of research at C.N.R.S., Institut du Quaternaire - Centre François Bordes.

SUD OUEST

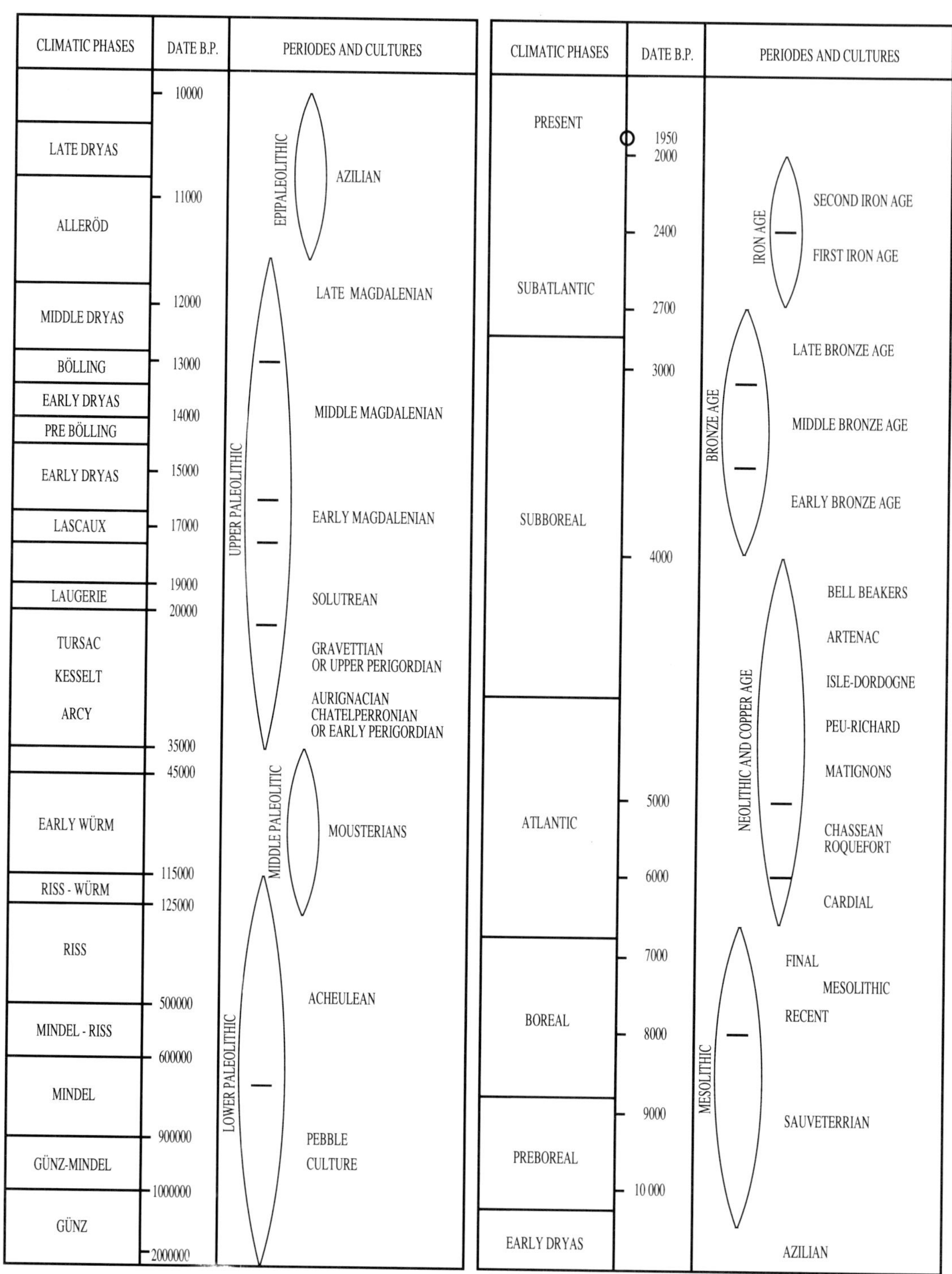

Chronological table of prehistoric and protohistoric times.

Geological time is divided into eras: the Primary, Secondary, Tertiary, and Quaternary. The Quaternary is marked by the presence of humans. This era is subdivided into three periods: the Paleolithic (lower, middle, and upper) or the stone age, the Neolithic or the polished stone age, and the Metal ages. Each period is broken down into several epochs which are essentially based on the kinds of stone or bone tools made by humans. It is this industry that serves as a basis for the cultural facies. The name of each epoch is derived from a large site which has yielded important vestiges of this time. Such a site is labelled "eponymous" wherein the Aurignacian is named after the site Aurignac, the Gravettian after La Gravette, and so on. The chronology established by carbon 14 dating is either presented in B.P. (before present) in which the "present" was set by convention to 1950 A.D. or according to "calendar dates" (B.C.) calibrated using other methods. The latter dates are older by a few centuries, since it was discovered that carbon 14 years are often shorter than calendar years. In the Paleolithic, dates are generally measured as "Before Present" (B.P.), since methods are not available to calibrate them otherwise. For the sake of consistency, the same dates are presented in the chronological table (above).

Frost from a cold winter whitens the area at the base of cliff in Les Eyzies, whereas several meters away, the heat of the sun reveal a recently plowed field. This same image evokes the notion of the glacial climate of the reindeer age, as it gradually give way to the milder times of agriculture.

Two or three million years: a brief summary.

Everywhere humans lived, they left behind a few bones, tools and weapons made of stone, bone,or metal, a few grams of charcoal, small pebbles, and virtually invisible grains of plant pollen. However, these odds and ends would be of little importance to us, if we were unable to breathe life into them.

Therein lies the work of the prehistorian (or protohistorian for work in periods closer to recorded history).

In understanding human history, one needs to be able to distinguish Christopher Columbus from Karl Marx, or Gutenberg from Napoleon. Understanding prehistory and protohistory requires a great deal of patience as one progresses step by step on the elusive paths of knowledge. Rosny's "Quest for Fire" mistakenly lumped together ancient humans, early hominids, Neandertals, and our immediate ancestors, Cro-Magnons. But these are successive periods, and we invite you to explore them with us in the Périgord region. It is here that, since earliest times, prehistoric and protohistoric humans have come to live.

THE DAWN OF TIME

The great age of our planet is truly staggering. Four billion years ago, the earth was formed. Life, a tiny blue algae, appeared 2 billion years later. Dinosaurs walked the earth and the first humans emerged only 2 million years ago in Africa. Only in the past 450,000 years have humans colonized the Périgord region of France. The Cro-Magnon rock-shelter was occupied only 30,000 years ago, and Lascaux was decorated just 17,000 years ago. In short, human prehistory is very recent. Now let us try to present it in an ordered perspective.

FOUR SUCCESSIVE HUMAN TYPES

Three million years ago, just prior to the emergence of the first humans, several small creatures appeared. They had poorly developed brains, walked erect, and subsisted by hunting. These were the Australopithecines of South and East Africa. One among them, Lucy, has become a big celebrity. Even her name was borrowed from a popular Beatles's song.

The first human was *Homo habilis* - a maker of stone tools. *Homo habilis*, who was also African and lived by hunting small, easily captured, prey (e.g. lizards, small birds) and gathering, and made pebblestone tools. These were used as much for cutting as they were for scraping, hammering, and digging. These handy humans were short (less than 1.5 meter high), their brains were rather small (650 cm3, or half that of ours), but the morphology of their bones indicates that they walked erect.

Their teeth also resemble our own more than they do those of an ape. They had no forehead, and possessed a heavy brow ridge that hung

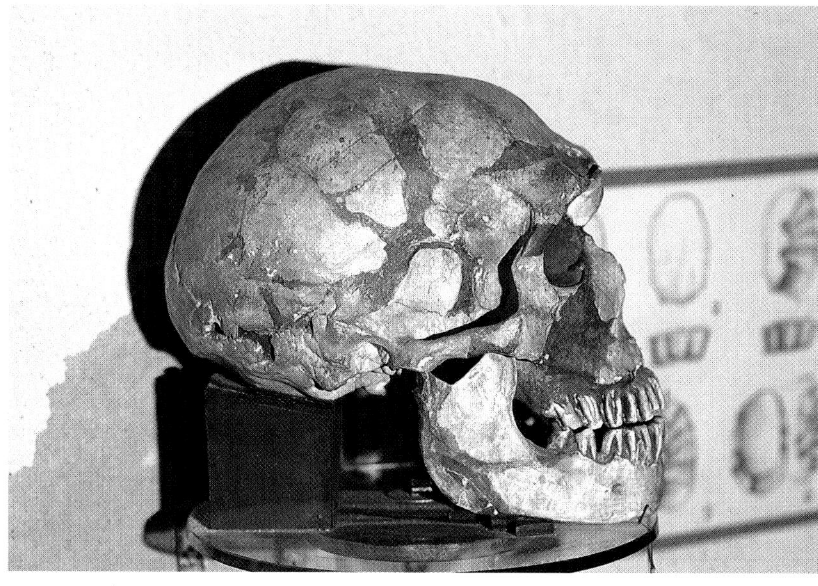

The first **Homo sapiens.** *This human skull, unearthed at La Ferrassie, did not belong to our direct ancestor, but rather a Neandertal which nonetheless is still classed among Homo sapiens. A few traits separate us from them: the shape of the skull, a sloping forehead, heavy, curved browridges, and an undeveloped chin. These skilled flint knappers also possibly had some spiritual orientation since they buried their own with care. In La Ferrassie, Peyrony discovered two adults and four children with ages ranging from ten years to a few days old.*

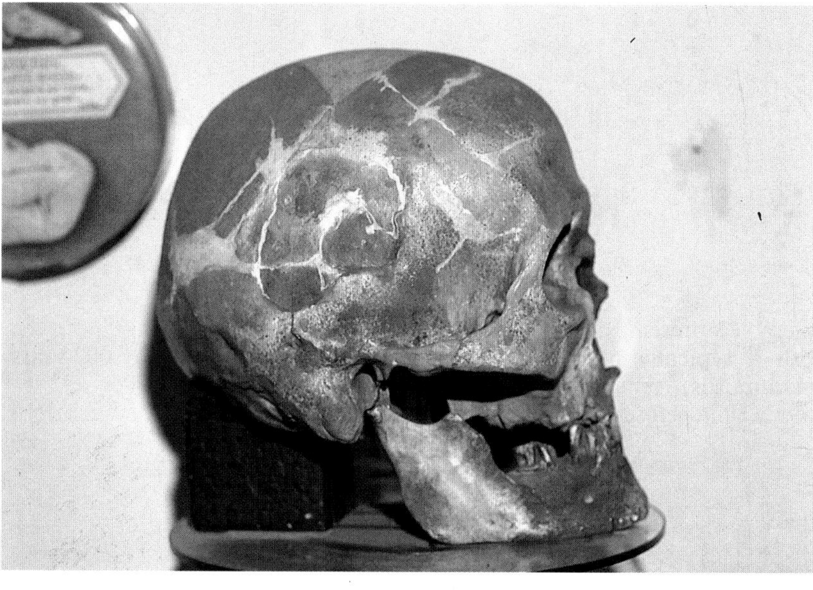

The first modern human. *This skull belonged to the most famous of our direct ancestors the people of Cro Magnon who were* Homo sapiens sapiens. *This was one of five individuals discovered in 1868 under the small rock-shelter of Cro Magnon near Les Eyzies train station. Nicknamed the "old man", he was probably no more than 50 years which was already quite old for this time period. This "race", or to put it more accurately, this type of human did not emerge first in the Les Eyzies region. Its predecessors were found in the Mousterian of the Near East. Thus, in the words of Yves Coppens, the people of Cro Magnon were thus migrant workers!*

over their eyes; their jaws were robust and without a chin. *Homo habilis* language is believed to have been very rudimentary. The color of their skin is, of course, unknown. They appeared in East and South Africa 2.5 million years ago and persisted for approximately one million years.

Homo erectus made their debut 1.5 million years ago in Africa, Asia, and Europe. The oldest French skeleton is of this type was from Arago cave near Tautavel in the Eastern Pyrenees. Erectus discovered the use of fire around 400,000 years ago. They lived in wind breaks made of branches, as in the case of Terra Amata, near the port of Nice. Their tool assemblage consisted of hardly more than a simple but ingenious tool type: the biface. It consisted of a rounded flint nodule, more or less flat and oval, with a cutting surface on all the edges. The biface was the all-purpose tool.

Homo erectus were no larger than their predecessors; their skulls retained more or less the same primitive characteristics, but their brains were larger (1000 to 1200 cm3, or a third of ours). The endocasts, taken of the insides of the skull, show that they possessed an articulate language. They were also hunters and even hunted mammoths (in the marshlands of Spain). In the hunt, they concentrated on archaic elephants, deer, wild boar, and small aurochs (wild oxen). This long period was marked by 'alternating cold and temperate climates. Some of the last *Homo erectus* occupied La Micoque site in Les Eyzies. These were the first "inhabitants of the Périgord", but skeletons have yet to be uncovered at his site.

100,000 years ago, new, somewhat rustic and robust humans appeared. They were slightly taller than their predecessors (1.6 meter) and had very large brains. They developed occipitals, sloping foreheads, and lacked chins. These were the Neandertals whose stone tool industry is known as 'Mousterian. Neandertals were no brutes; indeed they were the first *Homo sapiens* (which in latin translates to persons of wisdom and knowledge). They made superior tools such as impressive bifaces, but also scrapers, points, and blades. They collected fossils and minerals, and the presence of ocher and manganese crayons indicates that they developed an appreciation for colors. Near the end of this Mousterian period, they buried their dead in caves like La Chapelle aux Saints in Corrèze.

The last and most recent in this lineage were the Cro-Magnons who were every bit as human as 'ourselves. Indeed, we are all Cro-Magnons or *Homo sapiens sapiens*. We emerged 30,000 to 35,000 years ago and were no more or less attractive or intelligent than we are today. Naturally, Cro-Magnons did not have the same culture as we do. They manufactured tools from blades extracted from a large flint core (end scrapers, drills, burins, and points) and from animal bone and deer antlers (increasingly diverse forms of hunting weapons). They learned to sew, and made ornaments and a medley of other objects. They also quite suddenly began to depict by drawing and sculpting small figurines. CroMagnons appeared during the Upper Paleolithic, Neandertals were of the Middle Paleolithic, and the most ancient humans existed during the Lower Paleolithic.

An infinite number of caves. *Caves are a common phenomenon in limestone country where the rock is naturally broken by vertical or horizontal fractures which underground springs enlarged to carve out wide or narrow passage ways. These spaces were eventually filled in clay and calcite concretions such as stalactite, stalagmite, and flowstone. Humans used the entrances of caves as living sites or as a place to lay their dead. Cro-magnon, especially beginning with Lascaux's period 17,000 years ago, penetrated into the depths of cave galleries and passageways in the flickering light of their tallow lamps in order to decorate the cave walls. These decorated caves were religious places, underground sanctuaries. A few decorated caves like Saint-Cirq are rather shallow but the vast majority are represented by Gaume, Lascaux, Les Combarelles, Bara-Bahau, Villars en Périgord, Pech-Merle, and Cougnac in le Lot, Niaux in Ariège, and Altamira in Spain. Some, like Rouffignac, are immense and in the order of a kilometer deep. Today the galleries of this cave may be visited aboard a small train.*

WARM AND COLD SPELLS

Over the course of these millions of years, the climate was not always the same. Four long periods of cold called glaciations were interrupted by periods of warming known as interglacials. The two last glaciations bear the name Riss (500,000 to 125,000 years ago) and Würm (115,000 to 10,000 years ago) which were derived from two tributaries of the Danube where the glaciers in the basin of this river have been studied.

During these glaciations, the climate was clearly more rigorous than today (5°C cooler on average), and resembled present- day Scandinavia with a typically periglacial fauna (mammoths, reindeer, musk ox, woolly rhinoceroses, arctic foxes, and ptarmigans) and flora (a retreat of the forest and particularly deciduous plants, with only lichen, moss, a few clusters of willows, and dwarf birches during the extremely cold periods).

During these cold periods, the climate varied with latitude and altitude, proximity to the sea or mountains, from year to year, and from century to century. When the thermometer rose slightly, a marshland of alders, birches, and pines emerged in what constituted a taiga. A few degrees warmer produced a climate similar to ours and not unlike the interstadial of Lascaux 17,000 years ago.

A change in the fauna and flora followed accordingly Neandertals and Cro-Magnons lived during the Würm glaciation. However, it would be a mistake to imagine them living on some sort of icebank occupied by polar bears or suffering through blizzards and the long polar nights. They were not Inuits. The study of the animal bones (large herbivores, as well as small mammals and birds), plant pollens, and wood and mineral residues permits us to reconstruct the climate.

PLACES TO LIVE

From the earliest points in human prehistory, humans have built living structures - huts with frames made from branches (or even from the tusks of mammoths in the great plains of Russia which were covered by skins, and carpeted with furs). These structures were erected either in the open or ' 'beneath the overhang of a cliff that formed a rock-shelter or in the opening of a cave. *Homo erectus* at Terra Amata built a hut and even erected a small wall to protect themselves from the wind.

The Cro-Magnons, like us, sometimes even paved the floors of their huts as was the case in the lower Isle valley. However, these "cave dwellers" never actually lived inside these dark, humid, and quickly smoke-filled cavities. They often buried their dead in caves or ventured (sometimes quite far) into their depths to paint and engrave images on the walls.

The humans of the Paleolithic Périgord hunted, fished, and gathered their food. They lived the land without agriculture and husbandry. They led a life of semi-nomadic hunters, settling briefly in one area and then later moving on in search of game and reindeer in particular, which regularly travel long distances during their migration.

15,000 years at Abri Pataud (Les Eyzies). *The detailed excavations at the Abri Pataud in Les Eyzies have been used to reconstruct the very diverse climates which the hunters must have experienced during their fourteen principal occupations of the site. Conditions ranged from very cold climates (during which vegetation was sparse and the river was low) to near temperate climates that we experience today. Despite these variations, the occupations of the site roughly correspond to the coldest conditions in all the Quaternary (from 32,000 to 17,000 B.C.).*

***The history of France began with defeat.** The successors of Paleolithic humans saw the large herds of reindeer return to the north and the climate become milder. During the Neolithic, polished stone, and metal age, they also settled beneath rock-shelters, at the mouths of caves, or in open air locations. They buried their dead beneath dolmens and later in stony graves. Agriculture, husbandry, metallurgy, and ceramics did not emerge without kindling several less virtuous behaviors. Humans would forge the first weapons designed to defend themselves against their own kind and would build the first fortifications. By convention, the conquest of Gaulle by Julius Caesar and the end of the siege on Alésia in the year 52 B.C. marked the end of prehistoric and protohistoric times and the beginning of France's great history.*

THE GREAT RANGE OF ANIMALS

Not unlike the flora, the fauna also vary with the climate. During very cold periods, musk ox, mammoths, wooly rhinoceroses, reindeer, wolves, and smaller animals (weasels, hares, white foxes, ptarmagins, and snowy owls) thrive.

When the climate warms, a covered forest becomes home to mousses, bison, although reindeer, mammoths and wooly rhinoceroses persist. In the open clearings, large herds of reindeer, horses, and droves of wild oxen (aurochs) abound especially during seasonal migrations. Ibexes and chamois flourish on the high plateau, when they are not taking refuge in the high mountains. Felines hunt primarily at night, and cave bears retire to their caves to hibernate, drop their cubs, or die. (Caves bears were of the Mousterian period and were later succeeded by the brown bear in Cro-Magnon times).

What happened when the temperature rose a little more? Temperate forests appeared (with oak, hazel, Norway pine, junipers, and sometimes even walnut trees) intermixed with prairies populated by horses, aurochs, red deer, hinds, roe-deer, boars, and species of small animals that are still known today.

A historic excursion. *When they arrived in Les Eyzies in August 1863, Lartet and Christy descended upon this small cavity that was once called grotte Richard. A small fragment of an archeological layer from this, exhibited in Paris in 1862, inspired them to make the trip. Located in a cliff overlooking the Beune valley in Les Eyzies, this cave was occupied briefly in the Solutrean but predominantly in the Late Magdalenian.*

A fossilized living floor. *Hardened by the infiltrations of calcium enriched water, the archaeological level from grotte Richard can be cut into blocks or plates. Lartet and Christy sent samples of these to several museums including the Musée du Périgord. This "breccia" contains flint tools, cobblestones, animal bones - especially reindeer - that humans hunted and ate, and occasionally, small pieces of engraved stones or bones.*

Dates and People

Prehistory proceeded by trial and error for nearly two centuries before becoming recognized as a true science. Today, it is taught in our universities.

Several dates will illustrate the principal steps of this long path of progress from the early nineteenth century, humankind had not yet been recognized.

1810. A professor and occasional letter-press printer, F. Jouannet, explored Ecorneboeuf, a site which overlooks the modern city of Périgueux formed on the ancient city of Vésone. There, he collected flint arrow-points flaked and polished axes that he attributed to the Gauls.

1815-1816. Jouannet explored Pech de l'Aze cave near Sarlat, and Combe Grenal cave near Domme. In both cases, flint tools were found in association with animal bones. Jouannet wrote that "What we have seen bears the characteristics of the greatest antiquity".

1834. Concerning Badegoule cave near Le Lardin, the Jouannet suggested that a stone age existed that predated that of polished stones and of bronze, and yet Jouannet still attributed this stone age to the Gauls.

1847-1860. The publication of "Celtic and Antediluvian antiquities" by J. Boucher de Perthes officially marked the birth of prehistory thanks to geological, paleontological and archaeological observations made in the Abbeville region (in the valley of Somme).

1863-1864. E. Lartet, a magistrate in the Department of Gers, and Englishman H. Christy, Lartet's friend, patron, and manufacturer arrived in Les Eyzies in August 1863. For several months, they walked along the banks of the Vézère valley and explored some of the most prestigious sites: the grotte des Eyzies, the vallon of Gorge d'Enfer where one rock-shelter bears Lartet's name, Laugerie-Basse, Laugerie-Haute, La Madeleine, Le Moustier, and others. This period marked the beginning of an intensive period of excavations in the region.

1868. Several human skeletons dating to the Aurignacian period were uncovered in association with flint tools, beneath a small rock-shelter, near the train station in Les Eyzies. In 1874, Quatrefage and Hamy used these skeletons to define a new fossil race: Cro-Magnon.

1872. A skeleton was discovered near Laugerie-Basse which was also associated with bones, flint tools and also tools made of reindeer antlers. The same year, the French Association for the Advancement of Science visited Les Eyzies for its first conference. This date marked the start of archaeological tourism in the region. In 1883, The Joanne Guide had already begun describing the principal sites of interest in the region.

1874. This year saw the creation of the Société historique et archéologique du Périgord which to this day publishes numerous works on the region's prehistory.

1888. Féaux and Hardy exhumed a Magdalenian skeleton in front of the small Raymonden cave near Chancelade.

1895. Engravings and paintings were discovered in La Mouthe cave in Les Eyzies. They were found in a corridor which was uncovered at the base of the cave's entrance where Rivière had been excavating since 1894. It was the first decorated cave discovery in the Périgord, the third in all of Europe, after Altamira in Spain and Chabot cave in the Gard.

During the second half of the 19th century, several archaeologists excavated known sites and discovered still others. Gradually, a more exact chronology of prehistoric periods was developed (by Lartet, de Mortillet, and Piette). However the research methodologies were often too hurried and unorganized. A significant number of sites were destroyed forever. It was not until the 20th century that properly conducted excavations were undertaken, notably by D. Peyrony.

1900. Chance discovery of a small full-round sculpture called the "Venus of Sireuil" in the rut of a wagon track.

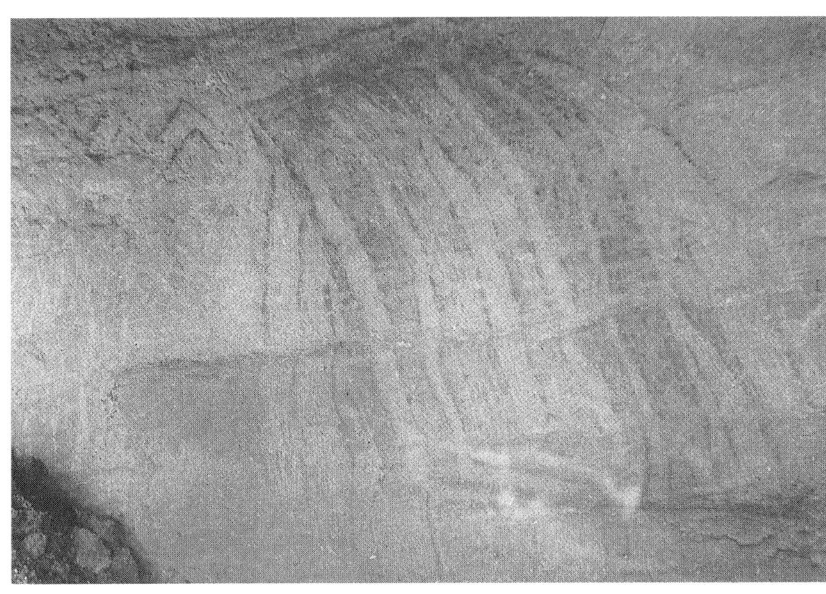

***A historic photograph.** This 1897 photograph was taken by E. Rivière in La Mouthe cave - the first discovered in the Périgord region in 1895. In order to insure that it not be published without his consent, Rivière printed it in blue making it impossible to reproduce at the time.*

1901. September 8. Capitan, Breuil, and Peyrony explored the Grotte de Combarelles where they discovered wall engravings. On September 12, Peyrony observed paintings and engravings in the cave of Font de Gaume. These two finds, in addition to the discoveries made at La Mouthe cave, contributed to the official recognition of the antiquity of cave art, which until then was questioned by a few archaeologists.

1908. A Swiss antiquary, who ransacked sites in the Périgord, found a Neandertal skeleton and sold it immediately to the Imperial museum in Berlin.

1909. At La Ferrassie, Peyrony, who had excavated there since 1902, uncovered one of the first of many Mousterian human burials. Others were found between 1909 and 1921.

1909. The excavation at the abri du Cap Blanc in Marquay yielded an animal frieze sculptured on the rock-shelter's back walls. It was the first discovery of wall sculptures.

1910-1913. Peyrony undertook a state funded excavation of La Madeleine where three phases of the Magdalenian are clearly defined.

1911-1912. Bas-relief representations of human beings were revealed in the abri Laussel near Cap Blanc but from an earlier period. In 1912, a sculpted fish was discovered on the ceiling of a rock-shelter in the Gorge d'Enfer in Les Eyzies.

1913. December 31. A law was passed concerning historic monuments, which guaranteed the protection of all present and future prehistoric sites. The same year, at Peyrony's suggestion, the government bought the ruins of the Château des Eyzies to convert it to a museum. The first exhibition opened in 1918, and the museum was officially inaugurated in 1923.

1921-1935. Peyrony excavated at Laugerie-Haute. This important site allowed the development of an exact chronology for several phases in the Upper Paleolithic and complemented the Ferrassie chronology.

1931 and 1933. Discovery of a cache of 27 bronze axes near Thonac. These finds were later protected by the state in 1943.

1934. Vidal found a Mesolithic skeleton at Roc du Barbeau near Le Moustier.

A few years before the Great War. *In 1908, a Bordeaux medical doctor and scholar, G. Lalanne, directed large scale excavations beneath the abri of Laussel, six kilometers up the Beune valley from Les Eyzies. This photo of the "dig site", taken in 1911-12, speaks for itself. However other archaeologists of the time, like Denis Peyrony, conducted more careful and meticulous excavations.*

1937. P.E. Jude exhumed an Azilian skeleton in the grotte de Rochereil near Lisle in the Dronne valley.

1940. Discovery of Lascaux cave which was authenticated immediately by the Abbé Breuil. Major alterations allowed Lascaux to be opened to the public by 1948.

1941. September 27. A law was enacted which influenced the regulation of archaeological excavations. Passed by the Vichy government and validated in 1945, it specified that all future excavations were subject to government authorization.

1950. Prehistory was introduced to the academic curriculum and later granted its own degree program in the Faculty of Science at the University of Bordeaux. The program was initially led by G. Malvesin-Fabre (1950-1956), followed by F. Bordes (1956-1981), F. Prat (1981-1989) and H. Laville (since 1989).

1953-1965. Professor F. Bordes excavated Combe-Grenal, a large Acheulean and Mousterian site.

1956. Led by Ch. Plassard, L.-R. Nougier and R. Robert discovered prehistoric drawings in the already well-known cave of Rouffignac.

1957-1959. F. Bordes and P. Smith excavated Laugerie-Haute.

1959. H. Delporte unearthed a female figurine in the excavations at abri Facteur.

1963. Lascaux cave was closed to the public when certain algal growth threatened the preservation of the paintings.

1967. F. Bordes reopened the excavation of Pech de l'Aze which he had initiated in 1948.

1968-1978. H. Delporte undertook the re-excavation and re-analysis of the large shelter of La Ferrassie.

1969-1981. J.-Ph. Rigaud excavated Grotte Vaufrey near Domme.

This is a sample of the dates that have marked the history of research in the Périgord. We have not been able to cite all of them here, nor have we included the more recent work which is either in progress or as yet unpublished. To this list, we might also add numerous discoveries of cave art, some of them quite recent, often made with the help of resourceful Périgord speleologists.

1. The Lower and Middle Paleolithic. From 450,000 to 35,000 years ago.

It is difficult to specify when the first humans occupied the Périgord. The discovery of primitive-looking tools in very old alluvial deposits has occurred here and there by chance, especially in the Isle 'valley. Some of these may have been abandoned by *Homo erectus* during the first two Quaternary glaciations (Günz and Mindel).

It was not until the third glaciation - called Riss - that true living sites are found in this region at Pech de l'Aze, La Micoque, and at Grotte Vaufrey where lower strata date to 450,000 years ago. These layers contain industries characterized by bifaces - stone tools worked on both faces - and tools made using retouched flakes such as points, scrapers, notched tools, backed knives, etc. These industries bear the name Acheulean (from St. Acheul on the outskirts of Amiens in the Somme valley where they were first defined in 1872).

Several varieties of Acheulean industries are defined on the basis of distinctive shapes of bifaces, the presence or proportions of certain tools, and the knapping technique used. Acheulean variants include Southern Acheulean, Clactonian (as defined by H. Breuil at Clacton-on-Sea in England), which is equivalent to the Tayacian described by Peyrony at La Micoque, Micoquian (which is a facies of Final Acheulean also found at La Micoque), and others.

A significant discovery dates to this Acheulean period - the controlled use of fire and the ability to light and maintain fires. This is confirmed by the numerous, organized, and structured fire pits that were discovered by François Bordes at Pech de l'Aze.

In the Périgord, no human remains have been recovered from this period, and the possibility of finding any is minimal since funerary rites and organized burials were not yet

A very old campsite. *Over 100,000 years ago, Acheulean peoples returned on several occasions to live at the base of a small rocky escarpment near the Manaurie stream, not far from the Vézère River. There are almost ten meters of archaeological deposits, the uppermost being a final Acheulean with elongated bifaces, with concave sides and finely retouched points. These are known as Micoquian bifaces.*

***An all-purpose tool.** The biface is a block of flint, cobblestone, or a large flake with retouch on two faces, more or less tapered on one end and more or less rounded on the other. The first bifaces go back to very ancient times in Africa. In Europe, they are typical of the Lower Paleolithic, and different forms characterized different phases. Variable in size, they may have served to break bones, cut branches, or possibly to scrape hides.*

practiced at least not in living sites. However, in the Eastern Pyrenees, the Caune de l'Arago has yielded several human bones including a large part of the face of a skull, and scattered remains mixed in with worked stone tools and animal bones.

Had the Acheuleans already developed a sense of aesthetics ? Many bifaces share a uniformity in size and regularity in form which suggests that the artisan went beyond the need to create efficient tools. Moreover, at Pech de l'Aze, a bovid rib bears engravings made with a flint tool. While the markings are not intelligible to us, they are clearly intentional and difficult to dismiss as the trivial diversions of an idle hunter.

In the Riss glaciation, a new industry appeared which differed from the Acheulean and bore closer resemblance to Mousterian industries found later with *Homo sapiens neandertalensis* in the Early Würm glaciation. Thus, at least in its beginnings, the Mousterian emerged as a technique rather than as an actual culture. This technique is found 200,000 years ago at Grotte Vaufrey, La Micoque, and is at times interstratified with the Acheulean.

The Mousterian appeared during the Riss glaciation and developed and diversified in the Early Würm between 115,000 and 35,000 years ago. It Le Moustier. In 1869, G. de Mortillet proposed to name comparable industries "Moustier Types" and in 1872 called the corresponding period the "Mousterian" (formerly written Moustierien).

Le Moustier, the eponymous site, was excavated more thoroughly in the early 20th century by Peyrony, and its industries were studied more closely around 1950 by François Bordes and Maurice Bourgon. The Mousterian forms an industrial complex composed of several distinct facies distinguished by their technology and typology. Bordes defined five major groups. Cordiform or triangular Bifaces were still present in certain cases (Mousterian of Acheulean tradition). There was a diversity of tools made from flakes composed of more than sixty, well-defined, retouched types of which points and above all scrapers were characteristic.

A means of knapping known as Levallois technique was developed in the Acheulean. This procedure consisted of shaping a block of raw material (a core), such that a flake of predetermined shape could be detached, then possibly adding retouch to make a tool. The presence of this knapping technique characterizes certain Mousterian assemblage types. The Mousterians occupied a wide area of the Périgord and often lived in open air sites, on plateaux, in valleys, and also beneath rock-shelters or in shallow caves.

Neandertals, who are considered to have already been *Homo sapiens* (*Homo sapiens neandertalensis*), lived in this period. They often buried their dead in organized and sometimes complex burials within living sites. Pits were dug, surrounded by stones, or covered with flagstones. Such funerary practices continued and diversified in the Upper Paleolithic.

A historic and prehistoric cave. *Located between Sarlat and Carsac, Pech de l'Aze is one of the earliest recognized cave sites, having been visited in 1815 by F. Jouannet. The cavity consists of a long corridor which passes clear through a limestone outcrop. While one of the extremities was occupied in the Acheulean and Mousterian, the opposite end or Pech I (photo right) was not occupied until the Mousterian at the start of the last glaciation.*

A complex excavation. *One hundred meters from the cave site of Pech I and Pech II, lies a large Mousterian talus site called Pech de l'Aze IV, which is situated against the cliff wall. It was discovered by F. Bordes who defined over twenty archaeological strata which in turn were further subdivided into several levels. At a such a site, it is difficult to excavate the same layer across the site's entire surface. Therefore the excavation was carried out in meter squares, and the data were recorded and regrouped stratum by stratum in maps and profiles.*

About 35,000 year ago, the last Neandertals were replaced by *Homo sapiens sapiens*. For a short period, called the Chatelperronian, the two groups may have co-existed.

LA MICOQUE

This famous site which opens to the southwest, is located on the right bank of the Manaurie channel, 500 meters above its confluence with the Vézère, just upriver from Laugerie-Haute. It is not a rock-shelter, but rather an open-air site at the base of a small limestone cliff about fifteen meters above a modern stream and a bank of river cobbles.

Discovered in 1895 by E. Rivière, the site was excavated indiscriminately by several archaeologists, especially by the antiquarian Otto Hauser from 1906 to 1914. It was nevertheless he who created the term "Micoquian" in 1916, to describe an industry peculiar to the site. This term was used again by Breuil in 1932, following excellent excavations conducted by Peyrony from 1929 to 1932, and after the site had been acquired by the state. In 1956, Bordes conducted a test excavation at La Micoque. In 1969, H. Laville and Jean-Philippe Rigaud completed a detailed stratigraphic study, and since 1983 a multi-disciplinary team of researchers has renewed an in-depth study of the site.

The statigraphic sequence at La Micoque is important to understanding the region's Lower and Middle Paleolithic, since the six successive occupations there correspond to the Riss and Early Würm glaciations.

The oldest Rissian industries, or even pre-Rissian industries, are in general composed of flakes which Peyrony attributed to Tayacian and Breuil associated with the Clactonian (levels 1 and 2). According to F. Bordes, levels 3 and 4, previously thought to be Tayacian, contain two Mousterian facies: one Quina (or Charentian), and the other Levallois. These two levels are contemporaneous with the Riss glaciation and thus are much earlier than the Early Würm glaciation which was formerly believed to correspond to the start of the Mousterian.

The top layer of the site contains Micoquian industries (Final Acheulean) characterized by elongated bifaces with wide bases, fine points, and slightly concave edges. This Micoquian tradition, at its eponymous site, is believed to date to the Early Würm glaciation.

PECH DE L'AZE

From Sarlat to Carsac, a road and an obsolete railroad track follow the small Font de Farge valley in which a now defunct stream once flowed into the Enea River, a tributary of the Dordogne. Four prehistoric sites are found at the foot of a limestone outcrop which crowns Pech de l'Azé hill (which means Donkey hill in the local vernacular).

Pech I and II are located at the two extremities of a 60 meter long cave which passes through a limestone outcrop. The first entrance is of historic importance because it was probably the first prehistoric site to be explored in the Périgord (by Jouannet in 1815). In the ' '1818 issue of the "Calendrier de La Dordogne", he described with astonishment the bones that had accumulated in the cave together with small fragments of black flint. Jouannet writes "How far back in time did this barbaric workmanship and unique deposits originate? We know not. If we speak of this cave in a work on the Gauls, it is only because all we have seen bears the characteristics of the greatest antiquity".

Later, a number of archaeologists visited the cave including Lartet and Christy in 1863. More recent excavations were undertaken by Peyrony in 1908, by R. Vaufrey in 1929, by François Bordes and M. Bourgon in 1948 and 1951. The latter two discovered the second entrance to the cave or Pech II. From this moment forward, Bordes dedicated several years to the excavation of Pech de l'Azé, explored a small nearby cave (Pech III), and discovered a vast collapsed rock-shelter, Pech IV, 100 meters downstream.

The entire complexe made a major contribution to a deeper understanding of the Lower and Middle Paleolithic, since the lower layers of the oldest strata were dated to the Mindel-Riss interglaciation and contain an Acheulean industry. The strata correspond to the Riss and Early Würm glaciations. During the same span of time, the climates, fauna, and flora varied with the climatic fluctuations from warm periods to cold or extreme cold periods in which reindeer were already quite abundant.

In Pech II, the incontestable presence of hearths demonstrates that humans controlled fire as early as the Acheulean. These were dug in the ground, sometimes surrounded by fire-reddened stones, and contained burned soils and blash ash.

An engraved bone was uncovered in one of these Acheulean strata, and several iron oxide and magnesium oxide chunks with scraping marks, were recovered from Mousterian strata. Some were even shaped into "crayon-like" implements. In one of the strata, Peyrony and Capitan also discovered an isolated crushed skull of a four year old child.

LE MOUSTIER

The small village of Le Moustier is perched on the point of a rocky promontory formed by the intersection of the Vézère River as it flows beneath La Roque-Saint-Christophe and the Vimont valley which descends from Plazac to the north. This promontory is accentuated by a series of terraces, the top one of which contains a small, shallow cavity - le trou du Bréchou.

Within the village itself the classic rock-shelter was explored in 1863-1864 by Lartet and Christy. It was this upper rock-shelter that later gave its name to the Mousterian period and industry. Ten meters lower, a second rock-shelter was excavated in the early 19th century, first by the antiquity dealer Otto Hauser in 1907, and then later by Peyrony after the French government purchased the site in 1910.

An eponymous site: Le Moustier. *Le Moustier is on the right bank of the Vézère at its confluence with the Vimont valley. Village houses rise in tiers on the rocky steps of the limestone outcrops at the angle formed by the two valleys. Two superposed rock-shelters have been excavated since 1863, and the industries found there have aided in classifying the Mousterian.*

A distinctive tool. *A small flint biface, a point, and a scraper from the eponymous site are the three "index fossils" of the Mousterian. But the tool assemblage of this period was not limited to these three implement types. Sixty other forms have been described. Aside from the tools themselves, the knapping techniques used to produce them and their relative proportions in the assemblage as a whole characterize the different facies of the Mousterian complex.*

A control section for the Mousterian. *Despite the numerous successive excavations at Le Moustier, one section of the rock-shelter's lower filling was preserved. Thus, we can see here the superposition of several Mousterian levels, below two Upper Paleolithic levels (Aurignacian and then Early Perigordian). In other words, occupations which stretched from about 50,000 to 32,000 years ago.*

Unfortunately for French archaeology, in August 1908, Hauser uncovered a human Neandertal skeleton which he named *Homo mousteriensis hauseri*. The remains were sold, at a high price, to the Berlin Museum of Anthropology where the skull was repeatedly - at reconstituted. It was believed that this skull was pulverized during World War II bombings, but the skull reappeared several years later in an East German laboratory (Iéna).

It might well be studied in more depth one day, but no reliable information is available on the burial itself. Today, we are more familiar with the human occupation of the higher rock-shelter and especially the lower rock-shelter, thanks to the excavations of Bourlon and Peyrony in 1905 and of Peyrony in 1910, and due to research on stone tool industries initiated by Bordes including the stratigraphic and sedimentological observations made by Laville and Rigaud in 1969.

The Mousterian occupation occurred in the two initial stages of the Würm glaciation and was followed by brief occupations in the Lower Perigordian and Aurignacian at a time when the two rock-shelters were nearly completely filled. In each occupation, the habitat also extended beyond the shelter's rocky overhang.

Peyrony, and especially Bordes, defined several types of stone tool industries characterized by tool types and their proportions in the overall tool assemblage. These facies do not seem to correspond to different populations but rather to varying activities

LA FERRASSIE

This site is somewhat off the beaten path, midway between Savignac-de-Miremont and Le Bugue, in a small valley which joins the Vézère at Le Bugue. Facing south, the large rock-shelter is at the intersection of the valley and a small vallon. The site sits at the side of a road whose very construction led to its discovery in the late 19th century.

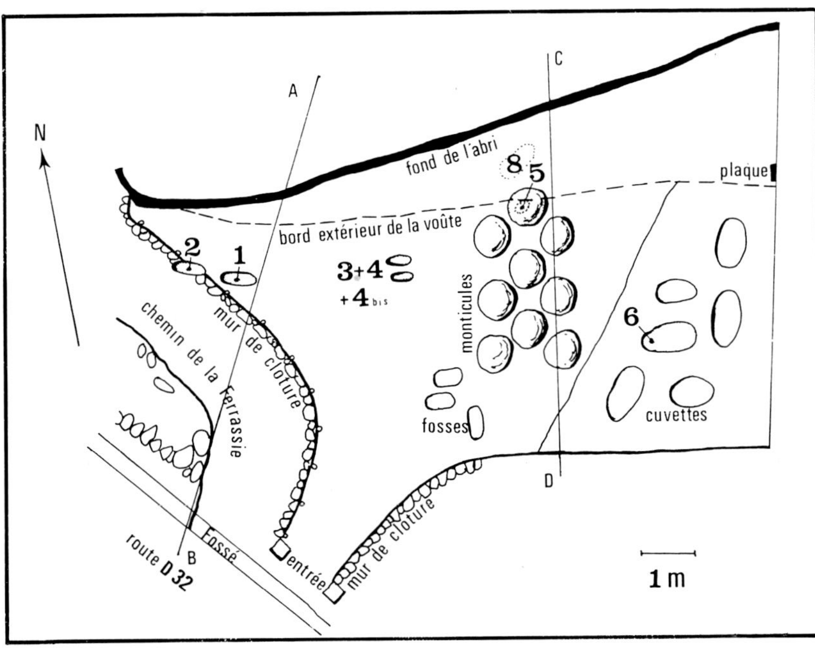

***A collective burial?** Between 1909 and 1921, Peyrony discovered several burials pits and mounds which appeared to constitute a structured arrangement, beneath the larger rock-shelter at La Ferrassie. Peyrony was not convinced that all the features were contemporaneous, although all the human remains from the Mousterian were Neandertal. On the left, there were two adults - a man and a woman; in the center, a 10-12 year-old child and two newborn infants; near the wall, a child of about seven months and a second of nearly two years, unearthed during more recent excavations by H. Delporte. Finally, on the right, in a pit covered with a limestone slab, a three year old child was found whose skull had been separated from its body at the time of interment.*

Very soon thereafter, amateur archaeologists made their way to La Ferrassie. These included Denis Peyrony, a young grade school teacher in Les Eyzies, who arrived at the site in 1896. For thirty-three years, Denis Peyrony made La Ferrassie his "home-base research site" in collaboration with L. Capitan who bought the site in 1923 and later sold it to the state.

The rock-shelter's overhang was invisible at the start of the research, because it was masked by a broad (40 meters long and 20 meters wide) talus. Little by little, Peyrony's excavations were able to reach the rock-shelter's fillings from successive occupations, as well as the large fallen blocks resulting from the regular collapse of the rock-shelter's overhang. By the end of the excavation, Peyrony had succeeded in excavating one hundred square meters of the site and had revealed the rear wall of the rock-shelter. Peyrony left behind two, six-meter, high stratigraphic profiles - one longitudinal and the other transversal.

Much later, between 1968 and 1973, H. Delporte renewed research at La Ferrassie. Starting from the control sections which he cleaned up, Delporte excavated only a small section of the archaeological filling but worked meticulously to clarify the details of the site's stratigraphy. As we shall see later.

La Ferrassie is a major site in the region's prehistory, especially in the earliest stages of the Upper Paleolithic, the Aurignacian and Perigordian. It was in fact at La Ferrassie and later at Laugerie-Haute and La Madeleine that Peyrony documented the successive human occupations of the Périgord. H. Breuil used these data on several occasions to establish his subdivisions of the Upper Paleolithic cultural chronology on a much larger scale.

La Ferrassie was the scene of significant discoveries for the Mousterian. From 1909 to 1921, Peyrony brought to light several human burials and various features associated with them. These remarkable finds made under controlled excavation conditions, made up for Hauser's disgraceful period in Le Moustier in 1908.

By the end of Peyrony's excavation, which was published in 1934, he was able to map all of the burials and associated features such as pits, depressions, and mounds, which are spread out over the entire explored surface.

On the left, two pits, each facing east-west, contained a 40-45 year old man and a 25-35 year old woman respectively. In another pit to the right, a 10-12 year old child was buried, and a fourth pit nearby held the remains of either a foetus brought to term or a 15 day old newborn child. In front of the rock-shelter, three empty pits and eight mounds were found. One mound yielded several bones of a seven month old child which was placed in a depression. Finally, one of the large depressions to the right contained the remains of an approximately three year old child whose skull was buried in a pit 1.25 meters from the body. The head was separated from the body at its interment or shortly before. In addition, this burial was covered by a large limestone gravestone bearing small pecked depressions. Delporte found a second

***A durable mandible.** Several skeletal remains were preserved from this Neandertal burial, including bones in the upper body, the vertebral column, and the sternum. However, no cranial material survived except this impressive robust mandible whose teeth were barely worn.*

child of approximately two years near the rock-shelter's wall near the mounds.

This is definite evidence of a funerary rite which was exceptionally complex for its time. It is also exceptional for the presence of young individuals whose ages range from newborn up to early adolescence. The remains of human adults contributed to a detailed study of neandertal characteristics. (The male is one of the best examples from this group). The remains of the younger individuals of various ages have contributed to an understanding of Neandertal growth and development. For example, it was observed that the maturation of the skeleton occurred at a faster rate than it does today, which accounts for the primitive characteristics.

REGOURDOU

The circumstances of the discovery of the site and of Regourdou's Mousterian burial are, to say the least, picturesque. Some five hundred meters from Lascaux, on the edge of the plateau overlooking the Vézère valley and the city of Montignac, Roger Constant, a resident of the small hamlet of Regourdou, aided the Abbé Glory in his study of Lascaux who even lived there on occasion. Convinced that an alternate entrance existed to Lascaux than the one currently recognized - which is well the original prehistoric entrance to Lascaux -, Constant excavated in front of his small farm. While he did not find an alternate entrance to Lascaux, he did discover a Mousterian site and a human burial in September 1957.

The Regourdou site is a vast rock-shelter site whose overhang collapsed after its archaeological filling. Following a chance discovery in 1957, the excavation was entrusted to two prehistorians, E. Bonifay and B. Vandermeersch, who worked from 1961 to 1965. Once the rubble from the overhang was cleared, they encountered several occupation levels containing Quina type Mousterian which was characterized by scrapers with flaked retouch and dated back to the beginning of the Würm glaciation.

The human burial was in a shallow pit, carefully capped by a flagstone and surrounded by a small wall of rubble. The body lay on its left side, the head facing North, with the knees bent under the chin and the hands brought towards the head. A fairly large sized limestone flagstone covered the trunk, while stone blocks and sand covered the rest of the burial. A fire was subsequently lit on this small burial mound, but it is unknown whether it is truly related to the interment.

A significant number of skeletal remains, including the sternum, were preserved. Unfortunately, the skull was not preserved but a well preserved and robust mandible was recovered with all its teeth intact and barely worn.

Adjacent to this human burial, there were also stone structures, paving, and lined pits or receptacles containing the bones and skulls of brown bears. In one deep and 1.5 meter-long pit, marked by small walls of stone and covered by a heavy flagstone, were the remains of a skull and bones of a single bear.

This complex ritual is very puzzling. The relationship between humans and bears (a bear cult) had already been suggested based on earlier discoveries in Swiss and Italian caves, although their ritual or religious interpretations were sharply criticized by A. Leroi-Gourhan. Needless to say, Bonifay and Vandermeersch's observations were controversial.

Le Cap Blanc (Marquay): a sculpted Magdalenian rock-shelter. *The occupation of prehistoric sites in the Périgord is not restricted to living sites, which at times are decorated by wall sculptures. As early as the Mousterian, Neandertals buried their dead. From the time of Lascaux, the Cro-Magnons lit the wicks of their lamps to penetrate deep caves where they decorated the walls and sometimes the ceilings. The arrangement of these depictions (whether painted or engraved,) the subject chosen, as well as the geometric signs which accompany them demonstrate that these were indeed sanctuaries or sacred places devoted to diverse religious practices and not simply magic as had long been believed.*

2. The Aurignacian and the Gravettian (or the Upper Perigordian). From 35,000 to 20,000 years ago.

Modern humans appeared some 35,000 years ago. The first 25,000 years of their existence corresponded to the end of the last glaciation called the Würm. This time period, the Upper Paleolithic, began with the Würm III - the coldest phase of this glaciation.

The oldest modern type humans, the first *Homo sapiens sapiens*, are commonly known as the Cro-Magnons. This name was derived from a rock-shelter situated in the village of Les Eyzies where the first fossil remains of these humans were found.

THE LAST MOUSTERIANS

The transition from the Middle Paleolithic was embodied in the Chatelperronian civilization (35,000 to 30,000 B.C.), which is known from Châtelperron cave in Allier. It is clearly defined at La Ferrassie above

The abri de Cro-Magnon (Les Eyzies). *This rock-shelter is located in the heart of the village of Les Eyzies. It was discovered in 1868, five years after the first prehistoric study was undertaken in the Périgord. In search of ballast to create a railroad track bed, workers unearthed the first known burial of borders the Vézère River's west bank, approximately 250 meters upriver from Abri Pataud, the site is today hidden behind the Cro-Magnon hotel, although signs and arrows direct the visitor. This small overhang whose ceiling collapsed at the time of excavation, was first a campsite for Aurignacians (25,000 to 30,000 years ago) before serving as a burial place. The human remains (at least three men, one woman, and a newborn child) were discovered near the top of the archaeological deposits which nearly completely filled the rock-shelter. One adult male who we refer to as the "old man" was no more than 45 years old.*

a series of Mousterian levels and beneath an Aurignacian sequence. The Châtelperronian is also present at the Abri du Moustier in Peyzac-Le-Moustier. It is a period in which the climate became progressively cooler.

This "Mousterian disguised as Upper Paleolithic", as Leroi-Gourhan would say, consisted of a combination of Mousterian type tools, a Mousterian-Levallois knapping technique, and Upper Paleolithic forms (burins and end scrapers). It is characterized by a tool with a curved back called the Châtelperron knife. At this time, the first true bone tools appeared which were essentially awls and a few sharpened bone antler fragments. The Châtelperronian layers at Arcy-sur-Cure in Yonne are famous for yielding the oldest bone pendants, the oldest bone with paired incisions, as well as Neandertal teeth. The discovery of a skeleton of a Neandertal male in the Châtelperronian at Saint Césaire in Charente-Maritime reinforced once again the notion of the transitional role this civilization played.

La Ferrassie's large rock-shelter (Savignac-de-Miremont). *Above the Mousterian strata, a succession of Aurignacian and Perigordian occupations yielded the very first evidence of prehistoric art - notably engraved, sculpted, or painted stone blocks.*

THE FIRST CRO-MAGNONS

The Aurignacian (about 32,000 to 25,000 B.C.) is the first of the Cro-Magnon culture. It was widespread in Europe (Spain, France, Central Europe, and Italy) and extended as far as the Near East. The excavation of several large sites in the Périgord (La Ferrassie, Castanet, and Pataud) served as basic references for all prehistorians.

The Aurignacians were subjected to an environment that alternated from harsh and dry climate with steppe-like grasslands to phases of increased humidity during which tree growth increased. Throughout this period, reindeer were the most common animals, along with horses and red deer (during less cold conditions) or mammoths and woolly rhinoceroses (when the climate became cooler).

A stone engraved with vulvar images from La Ferrassie. *This large limestone block (56 × 40 cm.) from the Aurignacian III bears two deeply engraved images of vulva surrounded by large depressions. Other dotted or finely incised lines may be traces of complementary images. Half of the drawings dated to the Aurignacian represent (predominantly female) sexual themes. From the invention of art on, Cro-Magnons mastered virtually all the techniques for stone decoration - engraving, sculpture, and painting.*

The Aurignacian tool kit. *In addition to the classic end-scrapers, burins, and perforators made on blades by all Upper Paleolithic hominids, the Aurignacians made a range of flint tools on thick blades, using a very characteristic scalar retouch. Scrapers were the most abundant. Changes in the morphology of their bone projectile points allows further subdivisions in the first important culture of the Upper Paleolithic.*

A painted ceiling broken in fragments (Abri Blanchard, Sergeac). *The Aurignacians at the Abri Blanchard also painted the ceiling of their rock-shelter, which collapsed due to frost during the coldest period of the Würm glaciation, thus shattering the decoration. On a large wall fragment, on exhibit at the Musée du Périgord in Périgueux, one can still read the black lines against a red background, which depict the limbs and ballooned stomach of an animal that probably represents a horse. The rest was destroyed. From 1910 to 1911, abri Blanchard was studied by Louis Didon and his trusty excavator, Marcel Castanet.*

***The Belcayre kid (Thonac).** The Abri du Renne of Belcayre is located less than a kilometer from the Vallon des Roches on the opposite (right) bank of the Vézère River, at the base of a row of collapsed cliffs. It was not excavated until 1923 or 1924, when Frank Delage found two Aurignacian levels. The most outstanding discovery was of a single block, decorated with the pecked image of an ibex. Shortly thereafter, the site was disturbed and the work was halted. Nevertheless, this ibex is of central importance among Aurignacian representations, since it is the only complete animal that has been well-dated. The animal's profile consists of stiff limbs and a lack of perspective. However, some details like the short tail and the small horns engraved on the edge of the stone block enable us to identify the species (Musée national de Préhistoire, Les Eyzies).*

Aurignacians developed implements which lasted throughout the Upper Paleolithic (end-scrapers, burins, perforators). But each period had its specialties. In the Aurignacian, end-scrapers were very abundant (more than 50% of the tools), blades were thick and sometimes narrow, and readily made using scalar retouch, which produced a large number of small flakes. Based on the composition of the tool kit and the shape of the bone points, an Early Aurignacian (I at La Ferrassie) is associated with split-based bone points, Middle Aurignacian (II at La Ferrassie) with more or less thick lozenge-shaped bone points, and a later Aurignacian (III and IV at La Ferrassie) with thicker bone points.

It was at this time that drawing was born. It was an extraordinary Cro-Magnon invention which consisted of reproducing in two dimensions what existed in nature in three dimensions. In Southern Germany (Bade Wurtemberg), Aurignacians invented the full-round sculpture. They representing animals and human beings. Here, in the Périgord, along the Vézère, and within a 15km radius of Les Eyzies, half a dozen Aurignacian camps beneath rock-shelters, yielded engraved or sculpted limestone blocks which were intermixed with artifacts of everyday life. The drawings usually consisted of female sexual images, rudimentary animals which were often incomplete, and puzzling geometric signs. In addition, since the beginning, humans decorated the overhangs or walls of their shelters with images made with strokes of paint, engraved lines, and applications of color. However, the extreme cold of the period, led to the deterioration of the walls exposed to the elements and as a result nothing is found in place today (Musée national de Préhistoire, Les Eyzies).

The oldest portable art object in France (Abri Blanchard near Sergeac). *The Vallon des Roches in Sergeac seems to have been a favorite place in the early Upper Paleolithic. Located on the right bank, Abri Blanchard was occupied on two separate occasions by Aurignacians (I and II). These occupants left behind about 15 decorated stone blocks. These are precious examples of the first representations of humanity and include female and male sexual signs (vulvas and phalluses) and animals deeply incised in limestone blocks. At the very base of the site, near a 30,000 years old hearth, was the oldest figurative art object to be discovered in France: a phallus made from the bony base of a bovid's horn. This object is currently preserved at the Musée des Antiquités Nationales, Saint-Germain-en-Laye.*

Our knowledge of the decorations stems from the fallen, identifiable, fragments that were recovered from the archaeological strata in sites like Blanchard, Castanet, La Ferrassie, Le Poisson, and Abri Pataud. Very few caves have decorations that date to this period. These caves are small with heavily eroded walls upon which an organized system of images can be seen. In Bernous, near Bourdeilles, three rudementary animals are aligned in a frieze, and in La Croze-de-Gontran at Les Eyzies, panels of animals are separated by geometric signs.

AND THEN CAME THE GRAVETTIANS

The Gravettian (25,000 to 17,000 B.C) is the second of the largest civilization of the Upper Paleolithic. It extends across Europe from Spain to Russia, all the way to the Don. But the largest number of known sites is concentrated in the Périgord. It is possibly for this reason that prehistorian D. Peyrony, founder of the Musée national de Préhistoire in Les Eyzies, designated this culture the Perigordian. He believed he could subdivide the Perigordian into six periods (I to VI). He later abandoned Perigordian I,II, and III, but continued to use the terms Perigordian IV, V, and VI to designate the unique stages of the Gravettian civilization. An additional stage was added to mark the terminal stage of the Gravettian - the Perigordian VII. At the time of its discovery at Laugerie-Haute, the Perigordian VII was called the Proto-Magdalenian by Peyrony. However, the name is deceiving since this industry, which is older than the Solutrean, does not belong to the Magdalenian sequence. Several famous Perigordian sites were occupied during the long periods of the Gravettian, among them the eponymous site La Gravette, in the Couze valley, La Ferrassie at Savignac-de-Miremont, and Laugerie-Haute in Les Eyzies. However, it was not until the excavation of the Abri Pataud between 1958 and 1964, that a complete stratigraphic sequence with all the Perigordian stages was revealed. As a rule, the term Gravettian is used to describe the civilization as a whole and especially its oldest phase. In the Périgord, the subdivisions are specified by using the terms Perigordian IV, V, VI, and VII.

The climate at this time was very cold. It was interrupted by several temperate episodes (such as the Tursac interstadial), during which tree growth resumed in the more open clearings.

A collapsed rock-shelter (Abri Labattut, Sergeac). *Located on the left side of the Vallon des Roches, directly across from Abri Blanchard, Abri Labattut gives some notion of a Cro-magnon habitat. 25,000 years ago, it was covered by a thin rock overhang that served as a roof and remains of it are still visible about two meters above ground level. The overhang collapsed and with it the wall art painted by Gravettians on the rock's surface. Several fragments were recovered from different living strata. One of them bore the contours of a red deer painted in black (Musée des Antiquités Nationales).*

A Gravettian hand (Abri Labattut, Sergeac). *The Abri Labattut served as a living site for the Gravettians on three principle occasions (Perigordian IV, V, and possibly VI). A block, which fell in one of these levels, preserved a hand print stenciled in black (Musée des Antiquités Nationales, Saint-Germain-en-Laye). It is the oldest known negative of a hand in existence along with those still covering the overhangs of Le Poisson rock-shelter in Les Eyzies.*

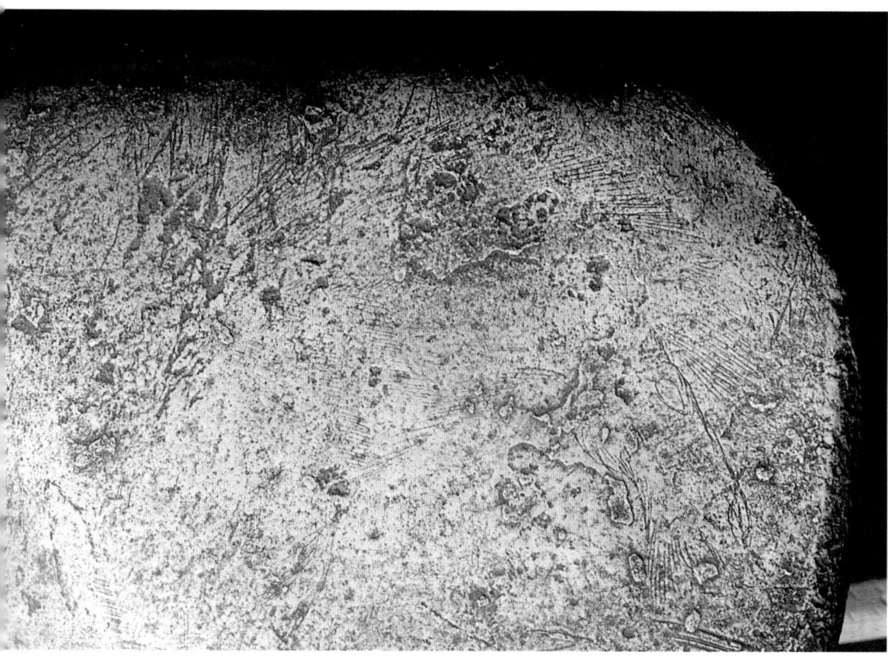

Engraved lines as fine as hair (Abri Labattut, Sergeac). *The Gravettians at the Abri Labattut left the most diverse examples of their artistic skills. One extraordinary, small (10 cm.), fine-grained, limestone pebble bears the finely engraved and carefully detailed image of a horse with a hatched mane, an eye, a beard, and hoofs. However, despite the abundance of detail, the style is still archaic with a ballooned stomach , short neck, long head, and lack of perspective in the limbs. The nature of the surface probably had a considerable influence on the quality of the image's details (Musée de l'Homme, reproduction by Sophie Delluc).*

The Gravettian tool kit. *In addition to the classic end-scrapers and burins found throughout the Upper Paleolithic, the Gravettian industry is characterized, in all strata, by the presence of Gravette points: straight backed blades, sometimes veritable darts, which were hafted onto the ends of very efficient hunting weapons. Other stone tools allow for further subdivisions to be made - the small Bayac arrowpoints ("fléchettes") in the Perigordian IV, and Font-Robert points, truncated blades and Noailles burins in the Perigordian V. The bone material is composed of awls and oblong bone points with or without a single bevel. The flintstones (left) were recovered in close proximity of the "Venus with the horn" (Musée d'Aquitaine).*

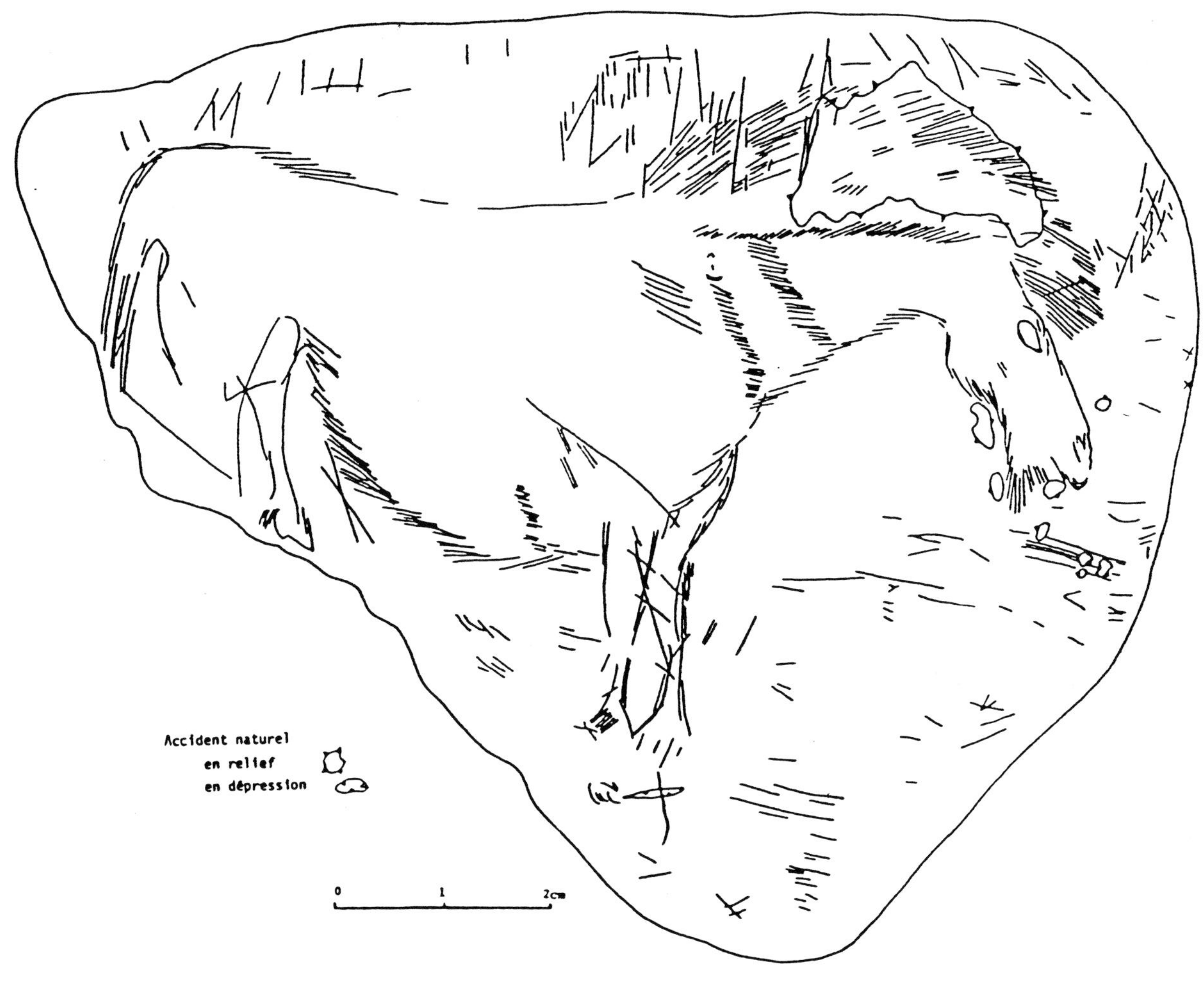

The flint tool assemblage became more diversified and specialized. Burins dominated (over 30%), followed by a large number of truncated burins, and relatively fewer end-scrapers. La Gravette points are present in every phase in variable proportions. Small arrowpoints are found the Perigordian IV, small Noailles burins, Font-Robert points, and some truncated elements in the Perigordian V, and long truncated blades in the Perigordian VI. In the Périgordian VII (or Proto-Magdalenian), the stone tools are composed of up to 40% burins and approximately 30% backed bladelets. Bone tools are always present but are not very characteristic (awls, pierced batons, and bone points) and ornaments are abundant (pierced shell, teeth, bone).

Cave art was still essentially limited to the walls of rock-shelters and associated with art on stone blocks, for which the Dordogne remained the epicenter. Nevertheless, during this period, two very remarkable caves were decorated: Pair-non-pair in Gironde and Gargas in the Pyrenees. The classic techniques of painting (as in Labattut) and engraving (from Oreille d'Enfer, Pataud, and Laugerie-Haute) were used, and sculptures (such as at Laussel and Le Poisson) became of considerable importance. Animal silhouettes were still rudimentary and in simple profile, but the species were identifiable. Sexual representations were present but appeared less frequently than in the Aurignacian. The female representations at Laussel are particularly spectacular. They correspond perfectly to the form of numerous, full-figured, female figurines called "Venuses" which have been unearthed in many Gravettian sites across Europe (Sireuil and Tursac in the Dordogne). Gravettian portable art includes animal figurines, finely carved pebbles, and some decorated tools.

LAUSSEL

La Grande Beune is a small, babbling brook which flows through a marshy valley. Several kilometers upstream from its junction with La Petite Beune, it passes between two castles. One is medieval and impressive in its austerity, while the second, Laussel, is smaller and less severe. The sites are located 500 meters upstream from Laussel castle and on the same river bank.

The Laussel site was most grandiose in the early 20th century when the woods and copse were still pristine. The Grand Abri stretches 100 meters and rises a dozen meters above the valley floor. It is flanked upstream by a smaller shelter, downstream by the Four (oven) rock-shelter, and is situated adjacent to a side wall which climbs abruptly to meet the Department highway 48.

Le Grand Abri was explored in the late 19th century and was later intensively excavated from 1908 to 1914 by Bordeaux native and prehistorian, Doctor Gaston Lalanne. The actual excavation, which was executed by local laborers, foreshadowed the trenches of the world war that would soon begin. Nevertheless, the site proved to be very valuable, both for its volume and the succession of eleven principle archaeological strata which stretched from the Mousterian to the Upper Solutrean. The discovery of depictions of humans in bas-relief underlined the site's importance.

The oldest deposits correspond to diverse facies of the Mousterian, followed by the classic succession of Lower Perigordian with Châtelperronian points, typical Aurignacian and Upper Perigordian with Gravette points, as well as several Font-Robert points. Finally, in the center of the shelter, two Solutrean levels were found. The superposed strata were five meters thick and 'were excavated alond a 48 meter long trench.

Laussel's renown stem from discoveries made in 1911 and 1912 of five sculpted human representations which seem to be from the Upper Perigordian layer, and consequently date to more than 20,000 years ago.

The most famous, the "Venus with the horn" was made on a stone block of several cubic meters which had fallen at the base of the shelter. It is classified as wall art. The other bas-relief art was made on limestone slabs of 40 to 50 centimeters in length and are classified as portable. All were found in a small area of the rock-shelter, within a few meters of the "Venus with the horn". The assemblage of art works suggests the existence of a sanctuary or *cella*.

Four of the five bas-reliefs are presently preserved in Bordeaux and exhibited at the Musée d'Aquitaine where they were donated in 1961 by members of the excavator's family. The fifth bas-relief was sold illegally to the Berlin Museum by a dishonest field director. Possibly destroyed during the second world war, all that remains are the copies at the Musée de l'Homme in Paris and at the Musée d'Aquitaine.

The "Venus with the horn", the "Venus with the gridded hair" and the so-called "Berlin Venus" all depict the frontal view of nude women with large breasts. In light of certain anatomical features, they probably represent women who have already been through several pregnancies. It is quite possible that the "Venus with the horn" was pregnant, given the size of her abdomen and the gesture of her hand on her stomach.

On the other hand, the profile of the "hunter" has long been described as male. While it has no breasts, it also shows no other male attributes, and it is quite possible that wide engraving which was pecked, rather than sculpted, two adjacent persons and inverted head to foot. One of the two is clearly female. Could it be a birthing scene?

Laussel... 50 years later. *The Abbé Breuil was photographed here by his partner Abbé Glory possibly in 1954. He was at the height of his career, a member of the Institute and known as the pope of prehistory. His first visit to Laussel probably dates to April 15, 1908, when he was 31 years old. At that time, he was part of a committee of eminent prehistorians from Paris, Toulouse, and the region which included E. Cartailhac, P. Raymond, the marquis of Fayolle, M. Féaux, P. Paris, D. Peyrony, and F. Delage. At Laussel and at Le Ruth the same day, the committee went into the field to verify the superposition of the Solutrean to the Aurignacian which until then had been contested by Gabriel de Mortillet and later by his son Adrien, to whom we owe the publication of the first periodical on prehistory in 1869. This visit and others in France marked the victory of the "battle for the Aurignacian".*

Mysterious "Venus". *This "Venus with the horn" from Laussel is the oldest known bas-relief depicting a woman. It appears that the woman is still fairly young but has already given birth a number of times. Her hand on her stomach hints that she may be pregnant again. In fact, many other sculpted representations, in full-round sculpture, from the same period, feature the same maternity theme.*

Hunter or Amazon ? *Not far from the "Venus with the horn" at Laussel, a slab of limestone bears the sculpted image of the profile of a slender person that had long been considered to be male and hence was named "the hunter". It is just as possible to interpret this image as a representation of a young female.*

GORGE D'ENFER

On the right bank of the Vézère River, the small valley known as the Gorge d'Enfer abruptly ends at the limestone massive which extends from Laugerie-Haute and the Grand Roc to Le Roc de Tayac. Seven prehistoric sites are found here in either caves or under rock-shelters scattered along less than 300 meters. However, this unusual concentration of sites corresponded to a very long stretch of time from the Aurignacian 34,000 years ago to the Upper Magdalenian 12,000 years ago.

On the left flank of the valley, Le Grand Abri is of impressive size at 40 meters deep and about 40 meters long. It was once the opening to a cave which was reshaped by thermoclastic erosion. While it was probably occupied in the Magdalenian, it was emptied of its archaeological filling by saltpeter mining during the French Rcvolution.

Slightly lower and downstream, Abri du Poisson and Abri Lartet were carved out of the stepped hills of a rocky outcrop. The former acquired its name from Edouard Lartet who discovered and excavated the shelter with his friend H. Christy in about 1863. Later in 1918, Peyrony uncovered an Early Aurignacian occupation at Lartet shelter which was characterized by split-based bone points and followed by a brief Late Perigordian occupation.

Just next door, Abri du Poisson was not discovered until 1892, and the sculpture of the salmon on the shelter's overhang not until 1912. That same year, the rock surrounding the sculpture was cut away in an initial attempt by the Berlin Museum of Anthropology to purchase the sculpture. However, Peyrony effectively intervened, the venture was abandoned, and the piece is still in place. Following this attempt, in which the sculpture was unfortunately damaged, the rock-shelter was quickly declared a historic monument.

The rock-shelter acquired its name from a large meter-long representation of what is incontestably a salmon (perhaps depicted in actual size). It is piked, that is, a male

A meter-long salmon. *This sculpture, made on the overhang of Abri du Poisson in the Gorge d'Enfer, represents a meter-long salmon which may be its actual size. It is the only sculpted representation of a fish, an animal rarely depicted in cave art, although it appears more frequently in portable art.*

The small valley of Gorge d'Enfer (Les Eyzies). *On the right bank of the Vézère River, slightly upstream from Les Eyzies, the small valley known as the Gorge d'Enfer was inhabited at several periods in prehistory, notably the Aurignacian and the Perigordian.*

The hinds of Oreille d'Enfer (Les Eyzies). *This block from the Musée national de Préhistoire in Les Eyzies depicts a group of four deer without antler (possibly hinds due to their large ears), with juxtaposed limbs which are not in perspective. This is a fragment from the wall of the Oreille d'Enfer (on the left bank of the small Gorge d'Enfer valley) which was removed for questionable preservation reasons. Its complement, which is still in place, is an exceptional assembly of shapes of animal tracks made with large pecked depressions surrounded by 2 or 4 small depressions. The site was occupied in succession by Gravettians (Noaille burins) - the authors of the engravings - and later by Solutreans.*

Opposite
Abri Pataud and Abri Vignaud (Les Eyzies). *Located 250 meters downstream from the Cro-Magnon shelter on the left bank of the Vézère, the site was discovered by Martial Pataud, a late 19th century farmer. However, it was American Prehistorian Hallam Movius from Harvard University who is credited with the exceptional scientific study of the Abri Pataud. The shelter itself has 9.25 meters of deposits in 14 successive human occupations including 9 Aurignacian levels, 4 very rich Gravettian levels or Perigordian IV, V, VI, and VII, and the remains of a Solutrean occupation with laurel leaf points.*
Behind the farm house, another very deep shelter was found. Today it is site of the Abri Pataud Museum. Signs of the site's use over time consist of traces of Gravettians and Solutreans including an exceptional bas-relief on the overhang; cave occupations in the Middle Ages, and a wall which was constructed in the 18th century. (The date 1734 was engraved on the lintel of one of the doors). Some 40,000 years ago, at the base of the cliff, at the present road level (rue des Eyzies), Mousterians camped on the banks of the Vézère. This site is called Abri Vignaud.

whose lower jaw is curved upward into a hook during the spawning season. The relief is very low and combines red and some traces are still visible in the grooves of the engravings. Above the fish, a square motif was hatched with seven lines. Below, another relief was carved, but its worn condition makes interpretation of the object difficult. Across from the fish on the same overhang, a negative of a hand stenciled in pale black was discovered several years ago.

The excavation carried out by Peyrony in 1917 and 1918, brought to light two successive occupations of this shelter - one in the Aurignacian as in Abri Lartet, and the second, in the Upper Perigordian. It is reasonable to assume that the wall sculpture and the painted hand were made during this later period.

Upstreaum from the Grand Abri, on the same side of the valley, a small cave is preceded by a rocky overhanging. The Oreille-d'Enfer or Les Chênes-verts cave was excavated intensively and anarchically in the early 20th century. The first "harvest" produced 300 kilograms of flint tools and bones. Two occupations were discovered, one from the Upper Perigordian with Noailles burins and the second from the Solutrean.

On a small flattening of the cave's wall, to the right of the cave's entrance, several engravings were unearthed from beneath the Upper Perigordian level. Thus, the engravings date at least to this period. Two nearly complete animals and the head of a third are represented. The engraving was detached from the wall and moved to Les Eyzies Museum to insure its preservation.

To the right of the removal scars, six related groups of pecked depressions are near a large central depression surrounded by three smaller ones. These designs are fairly comparable to those found in the Aurignacian of Blanchard, Castanet, and Laussel, and resemble the paw prints of carnivores such as the bear.

Opposite
The painted deer of Abri Vignaud (Les Eyzies): one of the world's oldest paintings. *The large fallen blocks upon which rest the terraces in front of the Pataud museum, once served as a shelter for a Gravettian hunting camp from the Perigordian V and is characterized by Noailles burins. One very large chip of rock was recovered during earlier excavations which showed that the wall was once painted. The piece bears the primitive sketch of a red deer painted in black with elaborate antlers.*

Mrs. Pataud (The Abri Pataud Museum, Les Eyzies). *This bronze statue was modeled after the skeleton of a young sixteen year old woman, who died 20,500 years ago and was buried at the back of the Abri Pataud with her newborn child (Level 2, Perigordian VII or Proto-Magdalenian). The young woman stood 1.6 meters high. She wore a necklace of beads and pierced teeth which were found next to her. She held in her hand a bone awl which must have served to pierced skins to be sewn together. The appearance of her clothing and her hair were the interpretation of E. Granquist, the sculptor.*

Female silhouette from the Abri Pataud (les Eyzies). *A small block bearing the engraved silhouette of a woman with atypical proportions was found. According to H. Movius, it came from level 3 (Perigordian VI) - a period which, approximately 21,000 years ago, corresponded to the coldest period of the Würm glaciation. The occupants built a veritable house between the cliff and the blocks of fallen rock. Or at least, this is the interpretation from the numerous artifacts left behind on their living floors which included hearths, the remains of prey, flint tools, objects of adornment, numerous art objects, and even debris from the painted decoration of the rock-shelter.*

The women of Terme-Pialat (Saint-Avit-Sénieur, Musée du Périgord). *As it was with the Aurignacians, women played a considerable role in the Gravettian artistic expression. They appeared less frequently in the form of vulvar images. Instead, their abundant silhouettes which were given little detail in the face, arms and legs in bas-relief (at Laussel or Term-Pialat) and in figurines (at Sireuil and Tursac) are quite famous. They are summarily labelled "venuses" and were found practically everywhere in Europe. They illustrate the spectacular cultural link that existed among the Gravettians throughout Europe.*

The engraved bison of La Grèze cave (Marquay). *This bison was engraved using deep but fine lines. It is executed in a primitive evident in its rigid pose in flat profile. The limbs (one per pair) are stiff and have no hoofs. But some detail began to appear as well (beard, tail, genitals, relief in the limbs) and the horns, though they are showing in frontal perspective an otherwise profile view, seem to be correctly placed below the nape of the hump. These features indicate that the image is more developed than those of Pair-non-Pair or Ardèche caves. This small decorated cave was illuminated by sunlight. Its entrance overlooks the Grande Beune valley. Early excavations uncovered Magdalenian and Solutrean flint tools like laurel leaves and shouldered points. The still rather rudimentary form of the animals, engraved in flat profile, the presence of certain anatomical details, and the absence of archaeological artifacts predating the Solutrean, place this small engraving in the Solutrean.*

3. The Solutrean and the Early Magdalenian. From 21,000 to 16,000 years ago.

THE DAYS OF THE SOLUTREANS 18,000-21,000 YEARS AGO

This splendid civilization existed only in a short time (18-15,000 B.C.) and space (in Spain and in the southern half of France between the Loire valley and the Pyrenees). It seemed to have appeared suddenly without direct links to the Gravettian (or the Upper Perigordian) civilization which preceded it in time and possibly originated in the Ardèche region.

Laugerie-Haute rock-shelter (Les Eyzies). *On the right bank of the Vézère, upriver from Les Eyzies, Laugerie-Haute extends 180 meters in length. It was explored in 1863 by Lartet and Christy, but Peyrony is credited with the first significant study of the site. Several successions of civilizations lived here from the Upper Perigordian to the Upper Magdalenian. The different phases are remarkably well represented. At the end of the Middle Magdalenian, the enormous collapse of the shelter's overhang sealed in the existing deposits.*

LAUGERIE-HAUTE

Laugerie-Haute (Upper Laugerie) is a little upriver from Laugerie-Basse (Lower Laugerie) which is how the former acquired its name. The entire cliff faces South-East and is thus well situated. However, from the road which borders the site, neither the shelters not their archaeological remains are visible, since they are masked by an enormous rubble which fell along the cliff's edge during the Magdalenian. Nevertheless, there is a vast living site, 180 meters long and a dozen meters wide, in the excavated area beneath the shelter. It is known that the living site once extended further into the valley under the present day road and beyond.

The art of flint knapping. *The people of the Solutrean excelled in the art of flint knapping, producing thin and sharp tools in the shape of laurel leaves with elaborate retouch.*

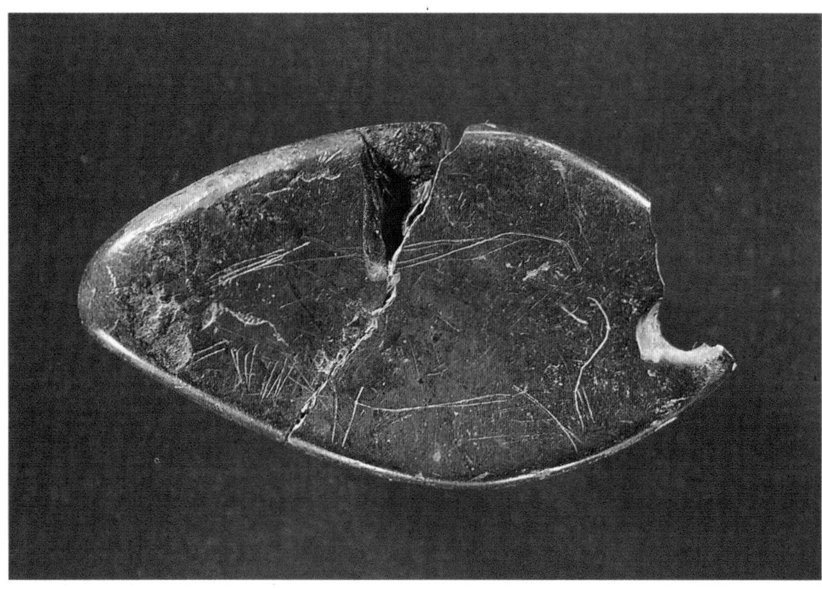

A lignite pendant. Le Fourneau du Diable (Bourdeilles). *This pendant is one of the rare portable art objects from the Solutrean. Made from lignite, a rare stone, it bears the engraved silhouette of a fairly rudimentary deer. The choice of material denotes the Solutreans interest in rare minerals. It is also known that they collected small shiny pebbles.*

The site is divided in two sections, Laugerie-Haute East and West, which are located on either side of a talus, upon which the old Chapoulie castle was built back in the 17th century. To the west, below the ruins of the Fournier house, several Neolithic human remains were recovered from the Magdalenian layer. This "skeletal shelter" is still private property, while the rest of the site has belonged to the state since 1921.

Lartet and Christy first explored, if not discovered, the site in 1863. Since then, Laugerie-Haute has prompted the interest of a number of archaeologists, enthusiasts, collectors, and profiteers drawn to its rich archaeological material, particularly Solutrean deposits with the laurel leaf - an impressive bifacial flint tool. Fortunately, after assuring that the site was acquired by the state, Peyrony and his son Elie were able to resume their scientific excavation and publish detailed observations in 1938. More recent developments at Laugerie-Haute include, work by Bordes and Ph. Smith which has added to our knowledge of the Upper Paleolithic, and G. Guichard's excavation of the site's eastern section.

Laugerie-Haute is a very important site in the general assessment of the Upper Paleolithic. Its stratigraphy begins where stratigraphies of earlier occupations at La Ferrassie and Abri Pataud end, and might have been succeeded by Laugerie-Basse in the Middle and Upper Magdalenian, had the latter been properly excavated. Instead, it is succeeded by La Madeleine for the last three phases.

At Laugerie-Haute, forty-two strata and levels were defined including various phases of the Final Perigordian, the Solutrean, and the first half of the Magdalenian. The Magdalenians V and VI were observed in old collections, but no objects are left in place. The sequence of intensive occupations of this vast rock-shelter represents a period of some 10,000 years and corresponds to a succession of several climatic phases which were meticulously analyzed by Henri Laville.

An ibex sculpted in bas-relief (Abri Pataud Museum, Les Eyzies). *In view of its style and the laurel leaves found on the ground beneath it, this ibex is definitely Solutrean. It was discovered in 1986 and today takes its place among the most exquisite works of prehistoric art. It was made in a similar fashion to the sculptures in Roc de Sers and Fourneau du Diable, and may date to 18,000 or 19,000 years ago. Note, however, that the rear limbs are simply juxtaposed and are not ' 'depicted on separate planes and in perspective like the forward limbs. This male alpine ibex (*Capra ibex*) is readily identified by its horns (the position of the left horn is unusual but not unique in prehistoric art). The small head, large belly, and short and animated limbs are in keeping with the style at Lascaux. This splendid sculpture was discovered on the ceiling of a rock-shelter, which, in the 18th century, was transformed into a wine-cellar and converted today into a site museum. This cellar was part of a farm built into the cliff in the small town of Les Eyzies. The Prehistoric site of Abri Pataud is located beneath the former Pataud barn and the old farm house currently serves as the site laboratory.*

The sculpted block from Le Fourneau du Diable (Bourdeilles). *This nearly half a cubic meter block is sculpted in bas-relief with animal shapes - two aurochs to the right and another oblique one in the center, as well as a barely visible horse further to the left. Other traces of animal forms or rough-outs are found in the upper right corner, and vulvar signs in the laurel are found in the lower right corner. The assemblage of animals must have been colored in red ochre, since a few traces still remain. These bovines with small heads, large bellies, and short limbs (and in one case with one ear laid in the nape of the neck) are quite typical of the Late Solutrean style which lasted into the Early Magdalenian at Lascaux. What is particularly remarkable is the respect for natural perspective which situates the two aurochs on the right, as well as the right and left limbs of the lower auroch, on two separate planes. By removing the rock surrounding the image, the animal's volume is accentuated in bas-relief against the background. The separation, however, was never completed and a small section of rock is still intact between the two aurochs heads. This stone block is on exhibit at the Musée national de Préhistoire in Les Eyzies and is comparable to bas-reliefs from Roc de Sers (Charente), which are from the same period, and currently on exhibit at the Musée des Antiquités Nationales in Saint-Germain-en-Laye.*

Laugerie-Haute is less rich in art objects than sites like Laugerie-Basse or La Madeleine, but some of them are of singular interest. The Final Perigordian or Perigordian VII produced a large 30 centimeter long gneiss pebble. Deeply incised groups of lines extending in several directions, forming puzzling motifs, are portrayed which must have been difficult to carve on the rock's hard surface. From the same period, a pierced baton (''bâton percé'') made from reindeer antler bears the engraved and light relief depictions of facing mammoths like those, more recent, found on the walls of Rouffignac cave. A sculpted piece of reindeer antler from the Early Solutrean which, according to Bordes, bears the head and body of a feline, was an exceptional find for this period. The backdirt from Hauser's excavations yielded a limestone sculpture of the head of an ovibos, or musk ox, with distinctive horns portrayed in front. The musk ox is rarely portrayed in prehistoric art.

ARTISANS AND TALENTED ARTISTS

The Solutreans were very skilled artisans and artists. They made high quality flint tools retouched on all surfaces. This technique lent considerable beauty to implements like unifaced points, laurel leaves, shouldered points, and willow leaf points. They also invented a tool used in life's daily routines: the eyed bone needle.

The Solutreans were also fine artists. In the early stages, they either in engraved or painted, (in black and red), the small caves of the Gorge d'Ardèche (grottes Chabot and Bidon) in a graphic style that became widespread in Lascaux times (such as the depiction of the bull's horns in twisted perspective).

A little later, in the Middle and Upper Solutrean of southwestern France, they decorated their sheltered living sites in bas-relief. Examples of these were found on the ceilings of the Pataud cellar in Les Eyzies, on the large blocks of stone at Fourneau du Diable near Bourdeilles and at Roc de Sers, between Brantôme and Angoulême. On a technological level, these sculptures were a culmination of Solutrean skills. Stylistically, they represent the emergence of high art, which 1,000 years later, was born and applied to the walls of Lascaux by the hands of the first Magdalenians.

One horse among hundreds (Lascaux, Abside). *This horse was engraved in thin angular lines using a sharp flint tool. It displays a Lascaux style with its small head, large belly, short and animated limbs, rounded hoofs beneath dew-claws, and fetlock hairs. But the entire image is more complex than it appears at first glance. It depicts 2 or 3 other horse heads, and three fronts and three rears are also portrayed. Are these the sketches of several superposed animals, or do they represent movement in a series of images? Stranger still are the superposed engravings of different signs: one of a partitioned rectangle and others in the form of long lines with thick midsections. The latter are called claviforms and are unique to the decorated caves of the Pyrenees and northern Spain. One of these signs forms the axis of a hut representation. The meaning behind these signs remains a mystery.*

A COMFORTABLE PLACE TO LIVE

Situated in the site of Fourneau du Diable and dating to the Late Solutrean, a remarkable living structure was uncovered. It consisted of a hut with a square base, surrounded by stones. The climate of this period was harsh, cold, and dry, particularly in the early and late periods of the Solutrean, interrupted by temperate, more humid climatic (one of which is best known as the Laugerie interstadial). Reindeer were abundant in the beginning of this period, and were followed later by ibexes and Solutré horses. With the exception of Solutré in Saône-et-Loire, the major sites of this time period are located in the Dordogne. These include Laugerie-Haute, Fourneau du Diable, Jean-Blancs, and Abri Pataud.

Few objects were decorated during this period, except in Parpallo near Valencia, Spain, which produced engravings on plaquettes of stone from the Gravettian to the Middle Magdalenian.

THE BADEGOULIANS AND THE FIRST MAGDALENIANS

The beginning of the great phase of the Upper Paleolithic is marked by the abundant bone industry and the quality and diversity of wall and portable art. This is the period of Lascaux.

The Magdalenian culture extended throughout Europe, but in the early stages, it was restricted to the French southwest and to a large site in Spain (El Parpalló near Valencia). The early sites were few in number and included Laugerie-Haute and Badegoule in the Dordogne (where it is sometimes referred to as Badegoulian), and Le Placard in Charente. The Early Magdalenian is not represented in the eponymous site of La Madeleine.

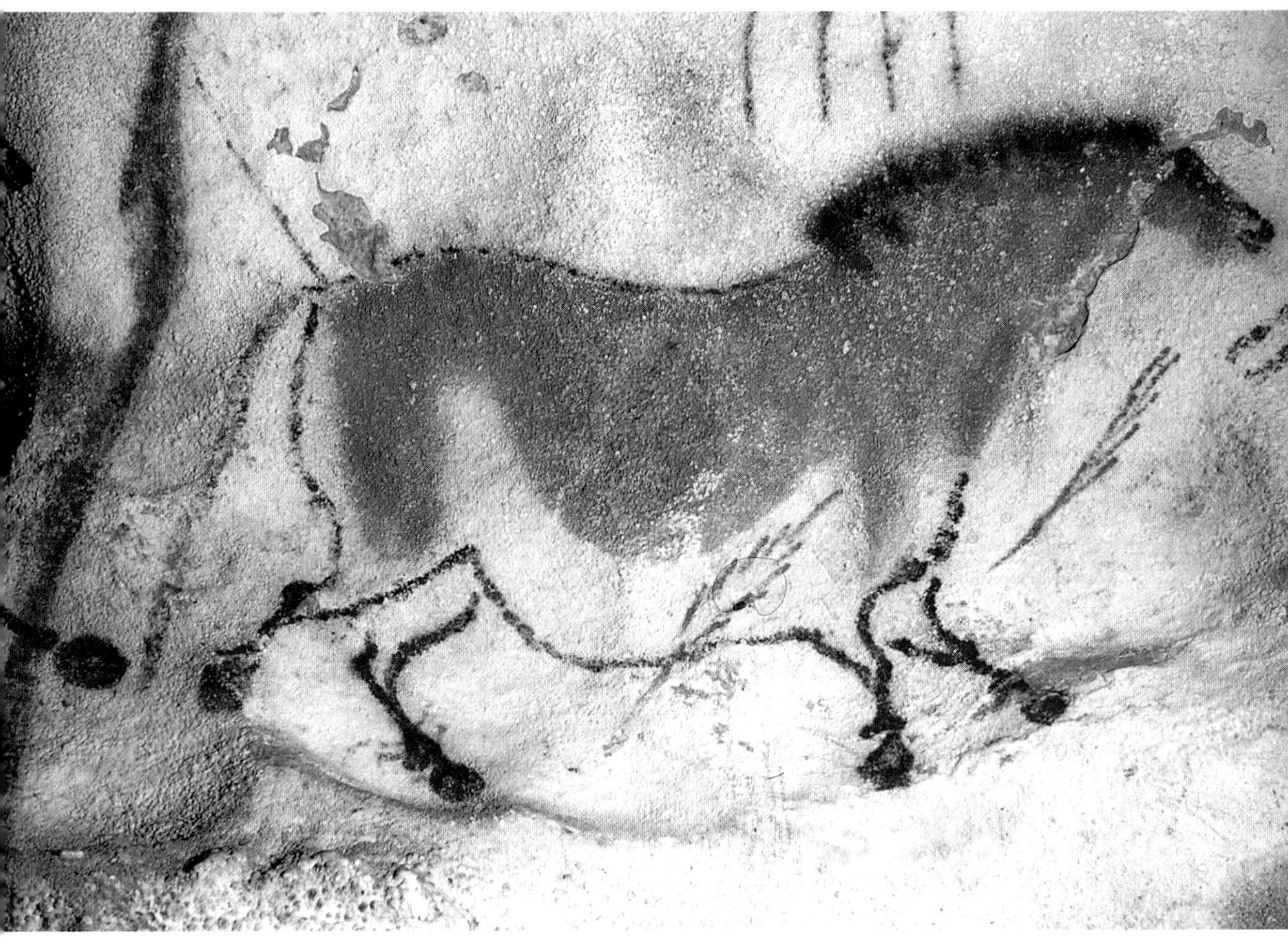

Another "very Lascaux" horse (Axial Gallery, Lascaux). *This 1.40 meter-long horse is very characteristic of the conventions of Lascaux artists: the small head, ballooned abdomen, short and animated limbs, the double line on the shoulder, the flat M-shaped coat, and dew-claws over rounded hoofs. The left limbs of the animal are separated from the body by a space which displays their position on a different plane. The raised mane, the light beard, as well as the coat and silhouette of the animal in general resemble the present day Przewalski's horse which is indigenous to Asia.*

Numerous geometric signs surround this figure. They are of three types; 1) filled signs - especially rectangles - which are usually partitioned like the heraldic coat of arms (featured here above the horse); 2) thin short stick-like signs which expand laterally to form anything from six pointed stars with lines centered at one point, or Saint-Andrew's crosses with lines bearing one or several barbs (see arrow-like figure in the lower right corner) to enclosed chevrons; and 3) punctuations forming solid or dotted lines. One last class of signs at Lascaux deserve mention here. These are claviforms (or club-like) and are normally found only in the caves of Ariège and northern Spain, which were decorated shortly after Lascaux. All of these signs relate a mysterious, indecipherable message. Several thousand years after Lascaux in the Middle to Upper Magdalenian, art became more realistic and less stylized than the types found at Lascaux. But the signs were still abundant. The cave and rock-shelter art of the great hunters of France and Spain disappeared some 10,000 years ago and reappeared later on open-air rocks (in the Arctic, the Alps, the Spanish levant, South Africa and the Sahara, Asia, Australia, America, etc.), often in a more schematic form than in prehistoric times and richer in human figures.

A SEPARATE CULTURE BETWEEN THE SOLUTREAN AND THE MAGDALENIAN

Today, many authors believe the Badegoulian culture, which emerged at the start of the Magdalenian, constituted an independent culture and a product of the Final Solutrean. It is characterized by a low number of backed blades and bladelets, an abundance of thin retouched flake scrapers, thick notched burins, and numerous flake perforators. The bases of the bone points have single bevels and hafting striations. Some bone implements are thick, and reindeer antler was worked using primitive percussion methods not practiced in the Magdalenian that followed.

THE FIRST TRUE MAGDALENIAN

The first Magdalenians continued to use the same basic tools of the Upper Paleolithic: blades, burins, and end-scrapers. But they also made dihedral burins, backed blades, small perforators, end-scrapers on unretouched blades, and composite tools (end-scraper-burins, etc.). Bone points had thick, conical bases and were decorated with a few engraved lines sometimes in the shape of stars or enclosed chevrons, (as in Lascaux). Harpoons had not yet been invented.

The climate was mild 17,000 years ago in the Lascaux interstadial but became cold and dry soon thereafter.

Horses and aurochs in the Hall of Bulls (Lascaux). *The association of a large bovine and several smaller horses is a common theme in Lascaux Art, and no doubt filled with symbolism. Unfortunately the meaning of this mythogram was lost. The contour lines of the bull are thick and retraced in red around the horns and withers. Near its forehead, lies a symmetrical pattern of dots and short lines.*
The decoration of Lascaux is very organized and patterned. It is like a cathedral with a carefully placed topographic distribution of subjects complemented by a language of geometric signs whose meanings still elude us. The art of Lascaux is unique. The anatomy and behavior of the animals are well represented, but their silhouettes are systematically deformed in keeping with the conventional style at Lascaux. The artist's hand corrected and transformed what was seen by the eye of the hunter. While this original art succeeds a more rudimentary form practiced by Aurignacians and Gravettians, it precedes the more realistic and more classical cave sanctuaries of the Middle and Upper Magdalenian. Lascaux is among the oldest of the cave sanctuaries. It is also the most original, the most beautiful, and the best known. During the explosion of Magdalenian art, Lascaux appears to be both a practice area for apprentices and a masters work. Like a "grand finale" which announces the "start" of a fireworks display, rather than signal its "end".

THE CONQUEST OF THE UNDERGROUND WORLD

One of the most remarkable events in the early Magdalenian was the invention or at least the expanded use of the tallow lamp - a natural stone with a slight depression or a carefully carved stone lamp made to form a receptacle. This event gave humans access to the underground world, where they decorated the first large sanctuary. This marked the beginnings of a Magdalenian artistic explosion for which Lascaux was the zenith, and soon meant an increase in the number of cave sanctuaries and art objects. However, apart from Lascaux - which was both a training workshop and a masterpiece - few decorated caves date back to this period, although one could cite Villars and Gabillou which resemble Lascaux in their style. From Lascaux's time forward, underground sanctuaries increased in number.

In single file (The Nave, Lascaux). *Five painted deer heads, each a meter high, form a frieze in The Nave. The artists must have atop the talus to gain access to this surface. The frieze consists of a group of fairly mature red deer depicted as one might have observed them in nature. The antlers are displayed in a conventional fashion, one before the other. Even the ears are depicted in a classical Lascaux style where one ear is tucked against the nape and the other against the side of the neck. The first four were drawn in black using manganese dioxide, while the last is maroon and was made using cave clay. The people of Lascaux did not eat these deer. Instead, they preferred reindeer which, save one, are not represented in this cave. An incomplete horse, which is difficult to discern, and a group of dots complement this composition. Though still unproven, the whole is thought to represent a river crossing. The reproduction of this frieze is on exhibit at Le Thot in Thonac, the Musée d'Aquitaine in Bordeaux, and the American Museum of Natural History in New York.*

THE LASCAUX SANCTUARY (MONTIGNAC) : THE PREHISTORIC SISTINE CHAPEL

The entrance to the cave sanctuary of Lascaux was blocked shortly after the cave was decorated 17,000 years ago by the first Magdalenians. This opening, which was reopened by a fallen tree, was discovered on September 8, 1940 by a young Montignac boy, Marcel Ravidat, when his dog had fallen into its depths. Marcel returned four days later with three friends (C. Agniel, S. Coencas, and J. Marsal) to widen the hole.

Lascaux cave is only 150 meters long, but its passageways are wide and high. The Hall of Bulls and the Axial Gallery were painted on hard, white, calcite walls. The rest of the cave (The Passageway, The Nave, The Apse, The Pit, The Chamber of Felines) was primarily decorated with engravings, and mixed paintings/engravings and paintings on yellowed limestone and sandstone surfaces.

Lascaux's floor had only one archaeological layer. Its contents included artist tools, flint and bone tools, objects of adornment, lamps, the remains of meals, pollens, charcoal, etc. These vestiges allow us to reconstitute the lives of those who frequented the cave and to date the works on the cave's walls. Methodical excavations would have produced better results, but the floor was summarily removed from the cave during initial cleaning efforts.

The resin on flint implements at Lascaux. *Some flint tools still bear the remnants of an adhesive on the side or face that served to secure a haft. It was not possible to analyze this adhesive in more detail, although it was probably made of powdered ochre and resin. The ochre was identified, but the resin, like all organic material, had decomposed and was not preserved. Still, this discovery gives us a clearer idea of how prehistoric humans used the tiny flint blades: they were hafted.*

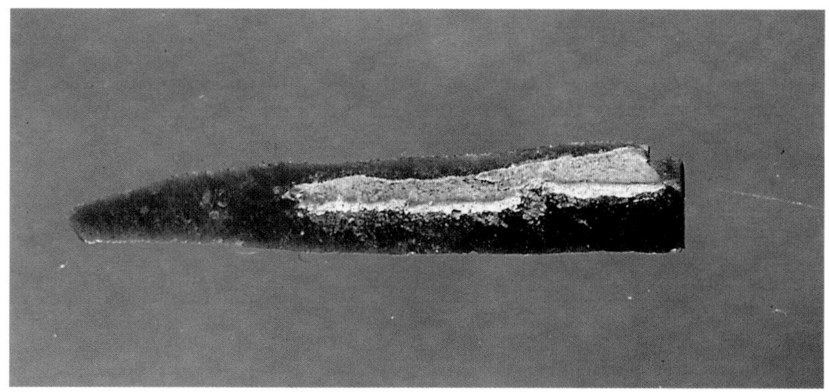

A sculpted, polished, and engraved, pink sandstone, lamp (The Pit, Lascaux). *This splendid object was found at the bottom of The Pit. A small depression in the lamp still contains some decomposed matter. This tallow lamp was used in closed quarters like our old oil lamps. Other lamps discovered in Lascaux include a lamp carved out of a limestone block and over one hundred lamps consisting of unaltered, flat, or slightly concave stones. Experimentation demonstrated that these stones, when supplied with a small dried-twig fire and a piece of tallow, worked like a candle in which the small fire would melt the fat upon contact. The charcoal would soak in the melted grease and from then on act as the wick. The amount of light given off by such a lamp, with one or several wicks, is equivalent to one of our candles. The lamps handle (for which the pink bears patterned signs which are unique to Lascaux. The same signs appear on one of the many bone points found in the cave's sediments as well as on the cave walls. This proves that the objects found in the cave's only archeological layer do indeed belong to the artists of Lascaux cave which dates to 17,000 years ago - the Early Magdalenian.*

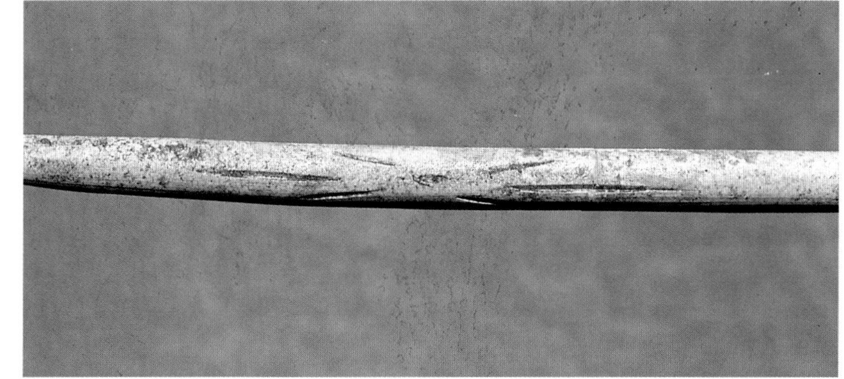

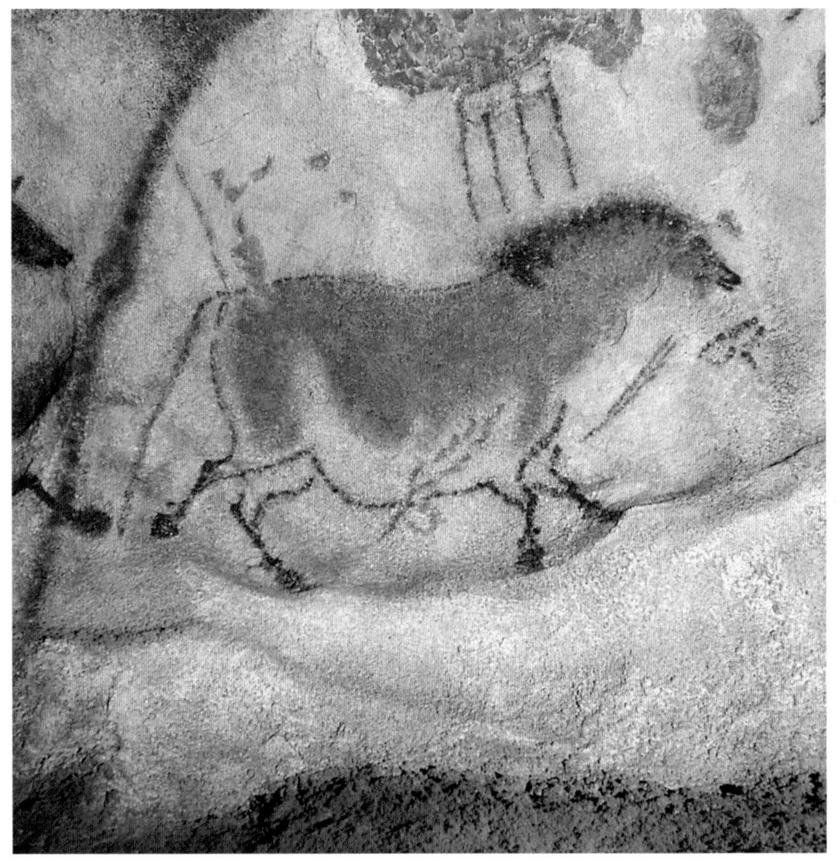

Object of adornment in the floor of Lascaux. *The people of Lascaux had a taste for adornment. Sixteen whole shells were discovered in the archaeological deposits. Three of them could be suspended on a string. Some originated from the Atlantic coast; other possibly came from the Mediterranean, and still others from the Tertiary layers of the Aquitaine or Tourane. This* Sipho *was pierced for suspension. It originated at the seashore and still carries red ochre in its spires - a pigment that was probably used to tan hides or to paint the skin of the man or woman who wore this gem. Lascaux even yielded a less exotic predecessor to our costume-jewelry: an oval pebble transformed into a shell by the addition of a few engraved lines which stimulate spires.*

A perfect copy: Lascaux II. *Since the preservation of Lascaux forced it to close its doors to tourism, two facsimiles were built. The first used actual size photograph-images which were applied to the reconstituted walls of the Hall of Bulls (on exhibit at the Saint-Germain-en-Laye Musée des Antiquités Nationales). The second was more ambitious and consisted of a copy of the Hall of Bulls and the Axial Gallery built underground near the original cave. Lascaux II is an iron reinforced cement shell whose dimensions match those of the original galleries. Its walls were painted with the signs and figures of the original cave with precise accuracy. The entire exhibit is preceded by two museographic panels that present the site's history, the archaeology of artifacts that allowed Lascaux to be dated, and the damage done to the cave since its discovery.*

Lascaux cave was a sanctuary. The organization and quality of its images, as well as the objects abandoned by those who frequented the cave prove that this was not the lair of some magician but rather a kind of cathedral devoted to one of prehistory's religions. Lascaux' artists were professionals who performed a service for the group and for the faith of its members.

The tourism generated by this decorated cave was formidable and almost resulted in the cave's destruction. Pollution, caused in part by the artificial recirculation of air, spread a green algae on the cave walls. It required that the cave be disinfected. The carbon dioxide, heat, and water vapors, brought in by tens of thousands of visitors each year, may have proliferated the opaque film of white calcite crystals which eventually covered the paintings. The dangers of this white disease caused the cave to be closed to tourism and attempts were made to recreate the microclimate which had preserved the art works for the past seventeen millennia. Only the future will tell whether this therapy was effective, but in 1983, a facsimile (Lascaux II) of the most spectacular parts once visited in the original cave was opened to the public. This also includes a museographic exhibit which shows the various objects found in Lascaux, presents archaeological arguments on the dating of the cave's art, and discusses the history of the cave's discovery.

In Villars as in Lascaux: a pictogram. *Prehistoric art lacked the art of storytelling. Few, if any of the animal figures, rare human depictions, nor signs represented in these cave sanctuaries tells a story. They are mythograms for which the meaning has been lost in the absence of an explanation from the person who once narrated them. Despite this, a few pictograms are still carry some meaning for us. These include the scene of a man and a bull (Lascaux, Villars, Roc de Sers), the battling ibexes (Lascaux), mammoths (Rouffignac), the parade of bisons back to back (Lascaux), and several other ethological scenes which demonstrate quite clearly that the caves' artists were hunters with a knowledge of animal anatomy and behavior.*

Here in Villars, a person holds its arms out in front. Calcite formation stands between the animal and the human figure. Another passes through the bison's back. Villars cave, near Brantôme, is an immense labyrinth, more than 10 kilometers long, with a great many concretions on its walls. In 1953, the Speleo-Club of Périgueux discovered the entrance. The paintings, which were found in 1958, are analogous in style to the images in Lascaux. However, they are fewer in number and often covered by a veil of calcite which gives the black manganese lines (used to draw the images), a steely blue tint. This too was a sanctuary and as in Lascaux, the scene of the human confronting a bison was made on the most remote panel of the cave.

48

A strange story (Lascaux, The Pit). *As the exception to the rule, this scene seems to tell a story. An eviscerated bull, with its intestines hanging, charges into a simple stick-figure human with a bird's head, four fingers on each hand, and an erect penis. Although, the animal is stiff, an unnaturally lowered head and a tail whipping about in the air give it some animation. Below, a bird seems to be perched upon a spear thrower and a barbed line may represent a bone point. Further to the left, stands a woolly rhinoceros across from which a horse was drawn. The bottom of The Pit contained a variety of objects, including lamps - one made of pink sandstone -, bone points, flint tools and pigments. Cave art, without exception, consists of juxtaposed images and signs, without any clear link between them. Narrative scenes, like this one (and in Villars cave and at the site of Roc de Sers), are very rare. Several facsimiles have been made of this famous panel and are currently on display to the public, notably at Le Thot in Thonac.*

***In the Beune Valley.** Today the vegetation partially hides the valley ridges once visible in the early 20th century. The excavation of Cap Blanc took place in 1909; the same year this picture was taken.*

4. The Middle Magdalenian. From 16,000 to 13,000 years ago.

It has become conventional to speak of the Middle Magdalenian which corresponds to stages III and IV of Breuil's subdivisions. Others would prefer to link stage III to the Lower Magdalenian and stage IV to the Upper Magdalenian.

This period is marked by a cold phase which lasted two thousand years, followed by a relatively milder climate. In the first phase, reindeer abound along with horses and saiga antelopes across a steppic grassy landscape. In the second phase, horses increased in number, while the antelope population decreased radically or disappeared. The climate became milder and more humid. Tree cover increased and even included deciduous trees.

The Magdalenian stone tool assemblage was fairly unremarkable with the usual procession of on the same blade or associated with other tools. Tiny retouched bladelets were quite numerous and were sometimes either denticulated or triangular.

Bone and reindeer antler industries are the key distinguishing features. Stage III is characterized by bone points which are often short and thick, with a single bevel, and generally with a longitudinal grove in the back. Semi-cylindrical antler segments also emerged at this time, often with either no decoration, or decorated with incised geometric signs. One also finds pierced batons, smoothing tools, notched bone, needles, etc.

In stage IV, bone points with single or double bevels, while sometimes striated, no longer bear dorsal groves. Antler segments are engraved or decorated with motifs in relief. Reindeer antler points also appear with lateral notches. These are often described as harpoon prototypes.

One also finds small, thin, perforated bone disks bearing geometric decorations or animal representations. Hooked spear throwers were made from reindeer antler or ivory, and were occasionally decorated with impressive full-round animal sculpture. The number of engravings on bone, ivory, reindeer antler, stones, pebbles, or plaquettes increased significantly in this period.

While defined at Laugerie-Haute, the Magdalenian III is also present at Cap Blanc, Reverdit, Raymonden, Gabillou and in some open-air sites in the Isle Valley. The Magdalenian IV was present in the lower stratum of the eponymous site, and at Laugerie-Basse and Raymonden.

THE CAP BLANC

The abri du Cap Blanc is located at mid-slope on the right bank of the Grande Beune valley, almost directly across from the powerful Commarque castle, the setting for R. Merle novel ''Malevil''. It was not until the beginning of the century that an excavator from the Laussel site, standing at the base of a small cliff, noticed a small crevice - a sign of a possible rock-shelter - and undertook an excavation on behalf his director, Dr. G. Lalanne. The operation was completed rather quickly. From September to December 1909, the entire site - fifteen meters long and three or four meters deep - had been completely excavated. When they reached the rock-shelter's rear wall, the excavators noticed the sculptures consisting of an animal frieze in high and low relief.

Horses emerging from the wall. *No one knows why the Magdalenians, who lived in Cap Blanc, sculpted this extraordinary frieze of horses on the wall of their rock-shelter. While it is believed that art had a magical or religious significance, it was placed here in a living site itself for all to see.*

A monumental work of art. *At Cap Blanc, this horse in high relief is more than two meters long. Despite some deterioration, it remains one of the masterpieces of cave art and is just one element of a nearly fifteen meter-long frieze.*

This monumental assembly is unique in the Périgord. No equivalent exists for this period, except at the abri du Roc aux Sorciers at Angle-sur-l'Anglin in Vienne. The composition is divided into two panels. The panel on the left is nine meters long and is located in the deepest recesses of the rock-shelter, while the second, further to the right, is four meters long and located in part on the ceiling of the rock-shelter's overhang.

Among the fourteen recorded animal represented, six are horses. All of them face to the right, save the most spectacular one in the center of the shelter which measures more than two meters in length. In two cases, a superposition of animals occurs where the head of the first is on the rump of the next. Three bison are also depicted among which one bison head was sculpted in place of a horse's head. A fourth bison was sculpted on a large now preserved at the Musée d'Aquitaine. A few other animals were more difficult to classify and are best left unidentified. Traces of red ochre are still visible in some places, which leads us to believe that frieze was once colored.

A study of the lithic and bone industries from Cap Blanc, preserved at the Musée de l'Homme and at the Musée d'Aquitaine, attributes the two principal layers of the site to the Middle Magdalenian (Breuil's Magdalenian III). It was during this period that the wall frieze was produced. However, there is some indication based on old collections, an excavation by Peyrony, and later from one of our own excavations, that the site was also occupied briefly during the Upper Magdalenian.

A human burial was discovered at the very base of the archaeological filling. It contained the skeleton of a young woman, about twenty years in age, who was laid on the left side in a flexed position. The heels almost touch the pelvis, and the right hand covers the face. Three large stone slabs were placed on the body. The skeleton currently on exhibit in the rock-shelter is in a different place from where it was discovered. The skeleton itself is a modern reconstruction, since the original was sold by the owner of the site to the Museum of Natural History, Chicago.

Thus, all under one rock-shelter, Cap Blanc shows a direct association among daily routine, funerary ritual, and splendid works of art which were possibly linked to the religion and rituals of the Magdalenian people.

__A bison rock-shelter.__ Here in Reverdit, three bison were sculpted for one horse, while at Cap Blanc the horse to bison ratio is six to two or three. Nevertheless, both sites are from the same period in the Magdalenian.

ABRI REVERDIT

In the Vallon des Roches in Sergeac, below Castelmerle, two rock-shelters were occupied during the Magdalenian. The first, La Souquette, is located on the left slope of the vallon and faces the Vézère River. The second, Abri Reverdit, is on the same side of the valley, only 300 meters upstream.

The latter derives its name from Alain Reverdit, an employee of "Administration des Tabacs". (Regulation board for the French tobacco Industry), who discovered it in 1875. Beneath the rock-shelter, which at the time was used as a stable or manger, he excavated what was left of the archeological filling. Later from 1911 to 1914, F. Delage reopened the excavation in front of the rock-shelter, recognizing that the prehistoric occupation had also extended towards the valley floor. The two recognized layers of archeological deposits were defined as Magdalenian III, just as at Cap Blanc.

It wasn't until around 1923 that M. Castanet, the owner of the site, discovered the sculptures along the overhang of the rock-shelter. In contrast to Cap Blanc, these sculptures are quite poorly preserved and occupy only a small section of the wall to the right, where a horse, two bison and the back of a third are portrayed.

In the left (or upriver) section of the site, a sloping talus abuts against the cliff face outside the rock-shelter and covers the remains of recently excavated archaeological strata. Several hearths appear in the control section, at the base of which another hearth, surrounded by large river cobblestones and placed on their sides in an oval formation, was uncovered.

__The famous "hut" of La Mouthe (Les Eyzies).__ Despite the nickname that was ascribed to this engraved and painted design, it is unlikely that it represents a prehistoric hut. The artists from this period did not portray objects or landscapes, only animals, humans, and puzzling geometric signs. This "hut" is one of these signs and is probably but attributed to the famous tectiform signs. These ethnic indicators are characteristic of caves in the Les Eyzies region from the Middle Magdalenian. The meaning of most of these signs is still a mystery.

The bison discovery: La Mouthe (Les Eyzies). *This engraved bison, depicted in great detail and in normal perspective, was the first engraved image to be discovered by G. Berthoumeyrou on April 11, 1895. It is located 100 meters from the entrance, on a wall of a small chamber surrounded by nine other bison, two ibexes, one deer, and various other vestiges. The style of these images is Lascaux type Magdalenian. The horns are longer than in today's bison and are shown at three-quarters perspective. Closer to the entrance, a small chamber features more rudimentary, if not more ancient, animals.*

In a little valley. *The residents of a small farm built a stable in a cavity in the cliff of the Vallon des Combarelles. From here, a narrow, long and winding gallery plunges underground and is covered with dozens of prehistoric engravings.*

The biggest of them all. *The Quaternary animal par excellence, the mammoth, is represented in Les Combarelles. At least 13 representations have been recorded which is few compared to the cave of Rouffignac, where they number over 154.*

LES COMBARELLES

Hurrah! As discoveries go, this one made of an immense engraved cave is big enough for both Capitan and myself. It is over 300 meters long and more than half its length consists of animal engravings, particularly horses, but also antelopes, reindeer, mammoths, and ibexes. It is just a dream come true. We happened upon it by chance, just as one might stumble upon something in the road. It is just too good to be true, especially when one has worked so hard for so long. I've traced 18 animals, and some of them are splendid indeed but are covered by a stalagmite film. Alas, there were far too many images, rather than not enough, and a number of beautiful heads are obscured. The profiles of some images were also outlined in black. This find is sure to shock the world of prehistoric art''.

This enthusiastic except was taken from a letter written by a young, Abbé Breuil to a friend and fellow school-mate from the seminary, Abbé Bouyssonie from Brive. It was written shortly after Breuil, along with Louis Capitan and Denis Peyrony, discovered the cave in Les Combarelles on September 8, 1901.

The discovery was a significant one indeed, since only five decorated caves were known to exist at this time. Curiously, some archaeologists were indifferent and even hostile toward the concept of cave art. The great antiquity of human beings had long been established, and numerous works of art had been unearthed and recognized as prehistoric. Still, many could not imagine that ''primitives'' were capable of penetrating the cave depths to practice their art.

The discoveries at La Mouthe in 1895 and at Pair-non-Pair (Gironde) in 1896 probably already planted the seed of doubt in the minds of the skeptics. The discovery of Les Combarelles, and of Font de Gaume several days later, was decisive. In May 1902, E. Cartilhac made honorable amends by publishing his ''*mea culpa* d'un sceptique'' in the periodical ''L'Anthropologie''. In August of the same year, a committee of specialists visited the three decorated caves in Les Eyzies and acknowledged the prehistoric age of the images. Numerous other discoveries made in the ensuing years revealed several new caves in the Périgord, the Pyrenees, and in Spain.

The existence of Les Combarelles was known prior to 1901. From 1891 to 1894, prehistorian E. Rivière had already excavated a rich site located near the entrance to the cave and the right gallery, called Combarelles II, where several engravings were found in 1934.

The main gallery, Combarelles I, is 240 meters long in its upper section. It is a narrow passage way with eleven bends and averages a meter in width but widens periodically at elbow level. After its discovery access was facilitated by lowering the floor, whereas originally, one was forced to crawl on a stalagmite floor filled with concretions to reach the engravings.

The diversity of fauna represented illustrates perfectly animal life in the Magdalenian. Included are rhinoceroses, bears, felines, and wolves. Horses were by far the most numerous with one hundred, and, according to Breuil, constitute a third of the engraved animal images. The next in order of frequency were bison, aurochs, bears, reindeer, mammoths, and deer.

Many human or anthropomorphic representations are intermixed with animal figures. A few very stylized depictions resemble the engravings at Lalinde or at Couze from the Upper Magdalenian. To this assortment, one must add signs, especially the tectiforms, the same as those found in Bernifal, Font de Gaume, and Rouffignac.

Based on their style, these works appear to stem from the Magdalenian, or more specifically the Middle Magdalenian; this according to A. Leroi-Gourhan, who did not exclude the possibility that some may be more recent and contemporaneous with engravings from Teyjat and Limeuil (Magdalenian V and VI respectively). In fact, a section of the layer excavated in 1973 in the chamber's entrance provided two carbon 14 dates. The oldest date was 11,730 B.C., the youngest was 9,430 B.C.

Feline number 52. *Soon after the discovery of Les Combarelles in 1901, Abbé Breuil committed himself to the task of tracing the cave's wall engravings. He succeeded in distinguishing 191 engravings depicted in 105 groups. Group number 52 associates a feline (the details of the head shown here), one upright rhinoceros, and a second depicted upside down and inverted head to foot with the first, surely a mysterious confrontation.*

FONT DE GAUME

In H. Breuil's words, Font de Gaume deserves to be ranked among the "giants" in cave art. While the frescoes covering the walls of the main gallery are not as bright as in Lascaux, and while they have sometimes been defaced by graffiti or covered by a veil of calcite, the high quality of the work emerges in the technique and style.

The locals had known of the cave's existence for some time. As Breuil amusingly explained, the cave was a favorite meeting place for young adults on their rendez-vous. The grade school teacher, Denis Peyrony, knew of the cave as well, and four days after an expedition to Les Combarelles, he decided to return there to look at the walls with new eyes. He was the first to see these "paintings of exquisite beauty" and eagerly alerted Breuil and Capitan who arrived on September 21st. For months, even years, Breuil regularly returned to Les Eyzies where, aided at times by Peyrony, he went about recording the paintings and engravings at Font de Gaume and Les Combarelles. The monograph on the former was richly illustrated with colors and published in 1910. The latter was published in 1924.

The cave was carved out of a large limestone outcrop, located five hundred meters from the right flank of the vallon of Font de gaume which opens on the left bank of La Beune. Starting from a sheltered porch that was remodeled in the Middle Ages, the main gallery is 120 meters long and noticeably narrow. Three galleries split off its right wall, one of which one leads to the outside.

The main paintings and engravings are located in the second half of the main gallery, just before the narro-

The entrance to the sanctuary. *The residents of Les Eyzies have always known about the grotte de Font de Gaume. They visited it frequently and unknowingly carved their names over the prehistoric drawings that went unnoticed. Just four days after the discovery of Les Combarelles, Denis Peyrony, then a grade school teacher, decided to return to Font de Gaume. There, he discovered and recognized the engravings and paintings covering the cave walls. The right gallery leads to the Magdalenian sanctuary, while the one to the left dead ends after a few meters.*

The cave of bison. *Some caves display a preference for certain animals. In Les Combarelles, it's the horse, while the mammoth is the favorite in Rouffignac. In Font de Gaume, it's the bison. Abbé Breuil counted eighty bison out of nearly two hundred images.*

wing passage named "the Rubicon", and continue along the high but narrow passage way until it dead ends. Several representations are also present in the second gallery and still others in the third.

Unlike Les Combarelles cave which was dedicated to horses, Font de Gaume cave was devoted to bison. H. Breuil counted 80 bison, 40 horses, 23 mammoths, 17 reindeer and deer, 8 aurochs, 4 goats, 2 felines, 1 wolf, 1 bear, and 1 human. To this one should add numerous signs, including 19 tectiforms and four negative (or stenciled) hands executed in color. The paintings are of exceptional quality. They are often bichrome or polychrome and superimposed upon a previously engraved representation of part or all of the animals. Time and time again, especially in the case of bison, the natural relief of the cave wall was used to suggest the volume of certain body parts like the head, hump, or limbs.

The animals are not randomly distributed. Some are associated in pairs such as two facing reindeer in a touching scene of loving affection. Others are portrayed in single file or organized in compositions. Some species occupy special positions. High on the cave wall, a wolf faces the intersection of the main and third gallery; a rhinoceros was painted in the last gallery, and an engraved feline at the very narrow end of the same passageway faces a group of horses.

A study of the styles and superpositions shows that the work was completed in several stages; one, more or less contemporaneous with Lascaux in the Early Magdalenian, and the other, in the later Magdalenian as found at Les Combarelles, Bernifal, and Rouffignac.

A strange sign. *An engraving of a house along with its floor, roof, and walls would be nothing less than unusual in the Magdalenian. It is quite unlikely that these engravings represent prehistoric houses. It was once suggested that they represented complex animal traps, but it is safer to interpret these engravings as signs whose meanings are unknown to us. It is, however, interesting to note that these signs are found only in the Périgord, including several here in Bernifal, and in Font de Gaume, Les Combarelles, and Rouffignac. This image possibly reflects particular cultural identity over a given period of time.*

Opposite :
Another tectiform sign was painted in the same cave (Bernifal). In normal light (above), one can discern the general shape of the painting, but when photographed on infra-red film (below), it is clear that the painting was made using a very organized series of small, juxtaposed, and evenly distributed dots.

BERNIFAL

Bernifal cave faces a hillside on the left bank of the Petite Beune, just downstream from the Vieil Mouly manor and mill, on the road from Les Eyzies to Sarlat.

In 1902, Denis Peyrony penetrated the cave through a small opening in the ceiling. He was not the first to pass this way, as testified by the graffiti made on the walls prior to his discovery of the paintings and engravings.

The cave was composed of two main chambers, separated by a very low and narrow passageway. Several small galleries which lead off from the second chamber, also conceal engravings and paintings in passages which are at times very narrow and barely accessible.

As in Rouffignac (but to a lesser degree). Bernifal is a mammoth cave. Mammoths constitute more than half of the 50 recorded animal representations. Most are engraved and the rest are painted including one which one deserves to be ranked among the best of the Rouffignac mammoths. Here, one finds a sense of style if not skill. Eight horses, including one ass, seven bovines (bison and aurochs), and two deer

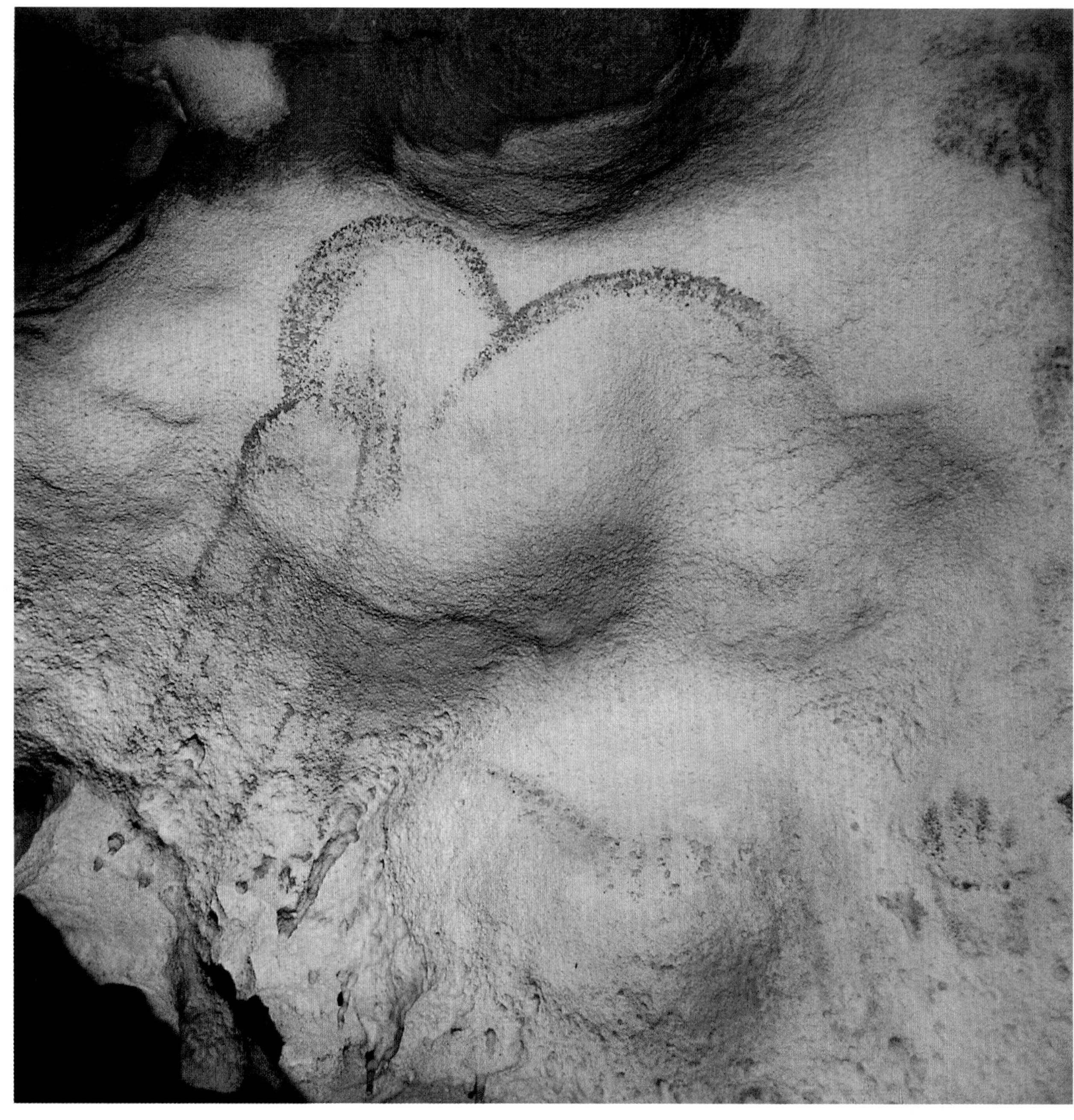

The hidden mammoth. *Engravings and paintings were uncovered in Bernifal cave as early as 1902. However, this mammoth was discovered only some 12 years ago. It was hidden in an almost inaccessible corridor, which had not yet been explored. In addition, its style was surprisingly similar to that found in Rouffignac. It was as if the same artist had frequented the two caves.*

complete the list of animals featured in the cave, which also has nine unidentifiable animals.

In one gallery, the natural relief in the cave wall resembles the profile of a human head. A few engraved lines made by prehistoric humans outline the nose, eye, and mouth.

Bernifal is also a tectiform cave. In the Périgord, these signs bear a strong resemblance to a drawing of a house with a gable roof, but it is unlikely that they represented living structures. There are thirteen such signs here. Twelve are engraved and one is painted using a series of small, juxtaposed dots. The engraved tectiforms are sometimes isolated, other times in pairs, and at times associated with mammoths. One animal that is absent here is the rhinoceros, while it is usually a counterpart to the mammoth in other decorated caves in the region. Like at Les Combarelles and Font de Gaume, there is at least one hand stenciled in black.

The cave of one hundred mammoths. *One often reads of "Rouffignac, the cave of one hundred mammoths". In reality, it would be fairer to call it the cave of 154 mammoths. Mammoths represent 70% of the animals featured in the cave. They are drawn in black or engraved on the cave wall. Mammoths appear individually, sometimes in pairs, and often face to face, even in groups of ten, in two opposing herds.*

ROUFFIGNAC

Rouffignac cave, also known as the grotte du Cluzeau, Cro de Granville, or grotte de Miremont, formed in a flint rich limestone outcrop, on the banks of the vallon of La Binche, just 5 kilometer as the crow flies from the Vézère River.

It would require many pages to recount the history of this cave which goes back to the year 1575. Rouffignac was the subject of what is probably the oldest known description of a decorated cave. In his Cosmographie Universelle de tout le monde (Cosmographies From Around the World), F. Belleforest mentioned "paintings and drawings animals". Over the last century, it was described in tourist guides as a center of interest. However, the discovery of prehistoric images dates only to 1956, when Ch. Plassard and two Pyrenees prehistorians, L.-R. Nougier and R. Robert, visited the cave and found these drawings.

Currently, 219 animal and four human representations have been recorded. This "cave of one hundred mammoths", as it is called in the tourist guides, in fact contains 154 mammoths, which constitute 70% of the animals represented in the cave. These are followed, in order of frequency, by 28 bison, 15 horses, 12 ibexes, 10 rhinoceroses, and a single bear. Thus, only six animal species are represented, but one of them in unusual proportions. Despite the fact that they are next to last in number, the ten rhinoceroses are of some significance, since in other caves they number no more than one or two.

Few signs are to be found in Rouffignac. Thirteen tectiforms and six serpentiforms - finger-engraved or painted wavy lines that resemble (or represent ?) serpents - have been recorded. Other signs include meandering finger-engraved shapes that appear throughout the cave and are called macaroni due to their pasta-like shape. These meandering lines cover the equivalent of five hundred square meters on the cave walls, especially on the cavity's ceilings.

Whether it be in black contour

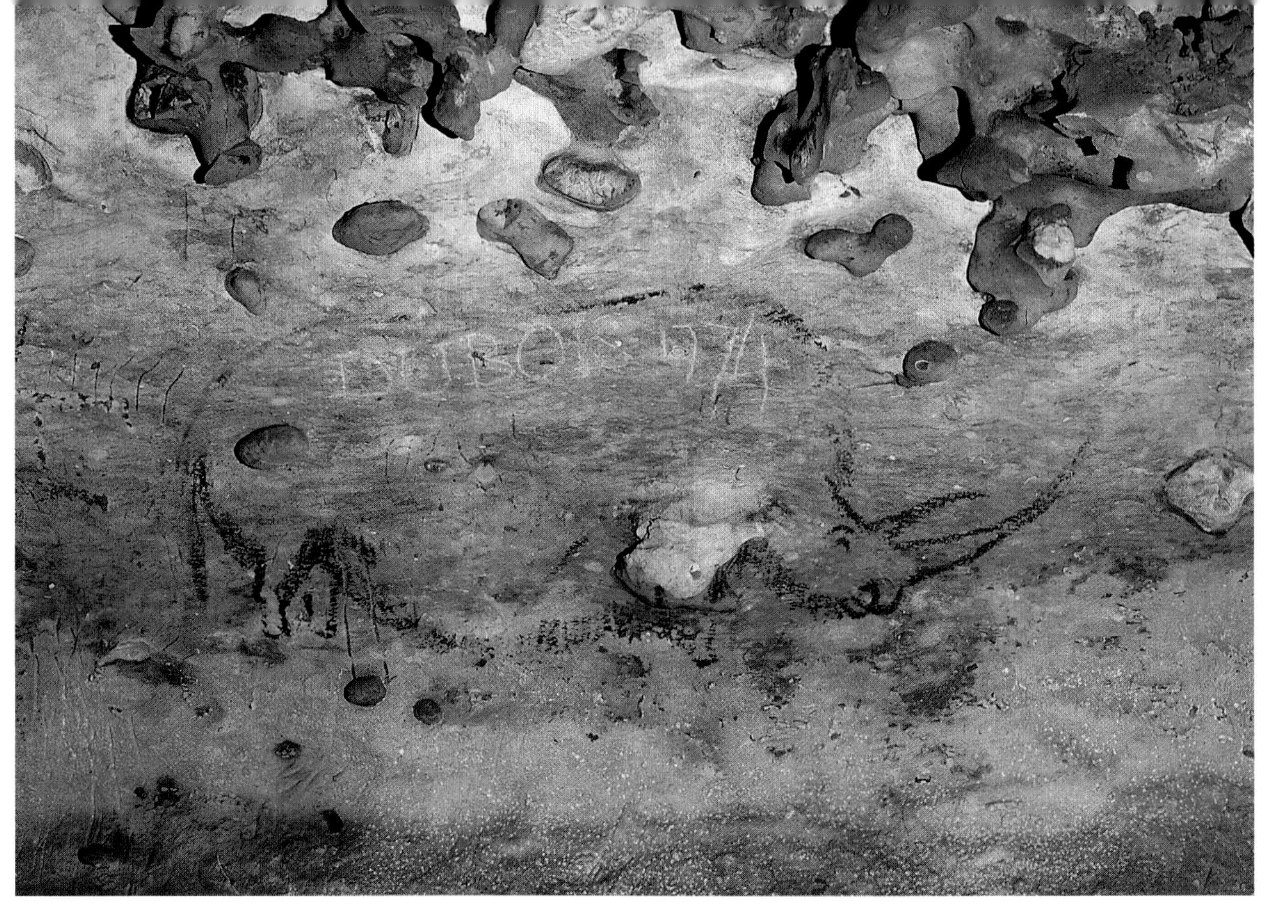

A dangerous herbivore. *Contemporaneous with the mammoth, the woolly rhinoceros is represented ten times in Rouffignac and is depicted in an extraordinary and particularly realistic frieze of three in a row. Very few representations of this animal exist. In the Périgord, however, a few have been found in Lascaux (the scene from the Pit), Les Combarelles, and Font de Gaume.*

paintings or engravings, Rouffignac's is an art form which, in most cases, employs a mastered skill of perfect execution to produce art of exceptional quality.

It is indeed curious that while the Magdalenians probably used the cave quite frequently, they left no material trace of their presence (such as worked flint, butchered animals remains, lamps, etc.). Only a single piece of worked flint was found in the pit beneath Le Grand Plafond. Nor is their any sign of a living site at the cave's entrance or in the immediate area. Where did the Rouffignac artists come from?

As in Lascaux and a number of other decorated caves, Rouffignac evokes the notion of sanctuary and art used as means to express spiritual or possibly religious throughts.

Due to the lack or archaeological material, the art style was used to date these cave paintings which were probably fairly late Magdalenian images. The great homogeneity of style and technique leads one to believe that a fairly small group of specialists from the same culture - one might even say from the same school - produced works within a set time span.

On the following page :
A 15,000 year old portrait of a man (Grotte Saint-Cirq). *Of course, this was not an accurate rendering. None of the prehistoric human representations were exact. Perhaps for religious reasons, the faces are either caricatures or devoid of detail. This individual was engraved in the rear of the small cave of Saint-Cirq and probably dates to the Middle Magdalenian. The engraving is located in a small depression in the cave's ceiling and is surrounded by several animal figures (ibex, bison, horse), a triangular sign, and two other human profiles. Despite the weak shoulders, the image represents a man. He is sometimes called the sorcerer, but this nickname has no basis whatso-ever. Several other animals - horses and bison - are engraved closer to the cave's entrance, and appear to date to Lascaux's period some 17,000 years ago.*

On the preceding pages :
Le Grand Plafond. *Near a pit that leads to a lower region of the cave, Le Grand Plafond in Rouffignac was decorated with sixty-three animal drawings. With the exception of the bear, all of the species found in Rouffignac are represented here, including mammoths, bison, horses, ibexes, and rhinoceroses. These animals are not depicted haphazardly. They constitute an organized circular composition in which horses and ibexes are arranged in a particular manner, while the mammoths appear to be more dispersed. This ensemble is even more remarkable when one considers that the floor was originally only 60 centimeters from the ceiling which made it impossible to see the entire composition at one time.*

A horse from Bara-Bahau (Le Bugue). *The rock which forms the walls and ceiling of this cave is nearly as soft as butter. It is littered with beds of flint in the form of large rounded nodules in the cave walls. Before humans arrived, bears - possibly large cave bears from the Mousterian - frequented this place. They scratched at the walls and left their distinctive claw marks of parallel rows of lines. The engravings, however, are more recent and date to the Magdalenian 15,000 years ago. This horse was engraved using a flint tool. Some lines around the head were made with the fingers. Some lines seem to depict the horses breath leaving its nostrils. The mane is raised as is the case in present-day Asian species. One can also see the hairs of its winter coat visible behind its shoulder. The hoofs were not depicted. A second horse was Could this be a depiction of a stallion-mare couple.*

The Bara-Bahau Cave (Le Bugue). *Bara-Bahau means crash or boom. This chalk cave owes its name to the enormous collapsed stone blocks which now litter its floor. It was called "grotte de la Cocagne" and was once a popular picnic site. At the rear of the cave, after 100 meters of a very wide and high gallery, a low passage way leads into a sanctuary decorated with engravings which form a frieze of horses, bison, aurochs, reindeer, and bear associated with tectiform signs. These signs and the style of the animal images enable us to place the decoration of this cave in the Middle Magdalenian which is the same period as Font de Gaume, Les Combarelles, Rouffignac, and Bernifal.*

5. The Upper Magdalenian. From 11,000 to 9,500 years ago.

With the end of glacial times fast approaching, large Quaternary animals such as the woolly mammoth and rhinoceros, as well as the migrating reindeer, began to disappear. This period was marked by a last bitter resurgence of cold temperatures in the Magdalenian V, followed by another cold but more humid period which gave rise to denser forests in the Magdalenian VI. Reindeer were still present, however deer, roedeer, wild boars, and aurochs appeared or increased in number and constituted the new fauna for the temperate periods to follow.

These last two stages of the Magdalenian are usually defined by the shape of harpoons made from reindeer antlers, whereby the Magdalenian V has unilaterally barbed harpoons and the Magdalenian VI harpoons are bilaterally barbed. However, an occasional harpoon with bilateral barbs may also appear in the first of these two stages. These objects served as the heads of harpoons. In other words, they were detachable weapons that were fitted onto a wooden haft. An unravelable cord probably enabled the user to recuperate the spear head and the harpooned prey. These objects often have widened bases which may have facilitated the tying of a cord and prevented the piece from slipping. Some more recent harpoons were even perforated for this same purpose.

The last stage of the Magdalenian also saw the emergence of new flint tools, notably parrot-beaked burins, points with semi-abrupt lateral retouch (Laugerie-Basse points), some with stems (Teyjat points). An increasing number of other forms were also developed that later served as the basis of the Azilian industry.

An exceptional site. *In the lower part of its course, the Vézère River makes a series of sinuous curves that meander from one side of the valley to the other. Slightly downriver from Tursac, it forms a near closed loop - or oxbow, called "cingle" in French - before flowing along the cliffs of La Madeleine at the base of which the type site of the Magdalenian is located.*

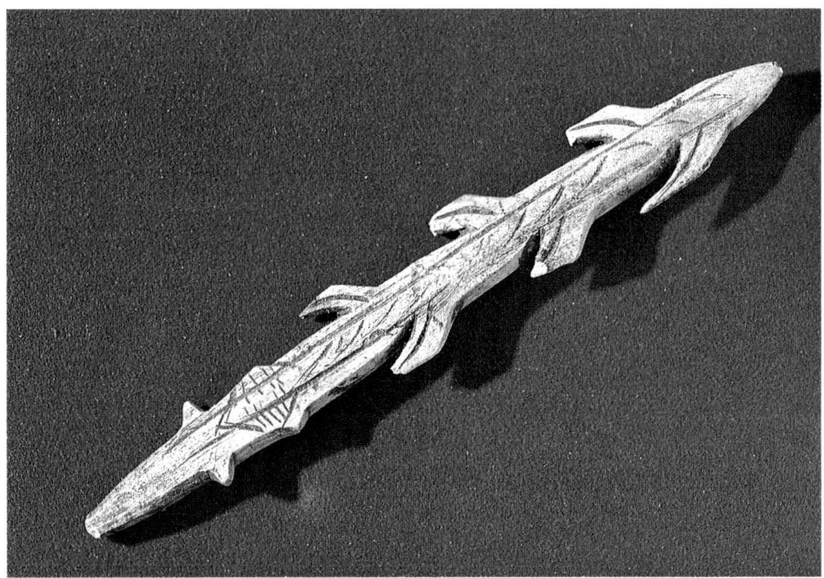

Fishing or hunting? *Magdalenian harpoons were generally made from reindeer antler and armed with barbs aligned along the edges. They were probably mounted on hafts which could then be flung using a spear thrower. It is not known whether these weapons were used to fish or hunt. Given the dimensions of the implements, both functions were possible. This harpoon comes from Rochereil (Musée de Brantôme).*

A masked human. *This bone fragment was discovered in the Magdalenian IV level at the base of the site La Madeleine. It bears an engraving that represents a clearly male human. However, the head is far from human but does not resembles the head of any known animal. It might involve a masked person, like others engraved on pebble from the same archeological layer (Musée national de Préhistoire in Les Eyzies).*

Such implements included Azilian points with curved backs and abrupt retouch, small and short end-scrapers, finely retouched geometrically shaped microliths, and a few flat harpoons from the extreme end of the Magdalenian. The latter were still made from reindeer antler and preceded the Azilian harpoons which were made from red deer antler.

This powerful culture was well represented in the Périgord and left behind works of art, mostly engravings, on cave walls (Teyjat), blocks of stone (Limeuil) and a number of other small objects such as bone, reindeer antler and stone. The art work ranges from rare artistic quality, and miniatures, to strangely deformed drawings of horses or reindeer with disproportionate heads, and very schematic or stylized pieces, notably the profiles of female figures.

LA MADELEINE

The Magdalenian is probably the most prestigious culture of all prehistoric times, particularly in the Reindeer Age, with its abundant reindeer herds.

In the course of their first archaeological exploration in 1863 to 1864, Lartet and Christy were drawn to a vast rock-shelter at the base of a cliff, on the right bank of the Vézère River at the water's edge. The site is unique. In the Tursac plane, the river begins a wide meander which snakes first against the rocky bore of Petit Marzac, then rebounds to the left bank of the valley, and returns to the same bore on the other side. It travels over two kilometers to end less than one hundred meters from its starting point! It flows at the base of the Petit Marzac castle and along the rock-shelter and then snakes away in the direction of Les Eyzies.

The excavated area of the site is 50 meters long and 10 to 15 meters wide. Lartet and Christy excavated the central zone which is at least 2.5 meters thick. In May 1864, the discovery of a large piece of mammoth tusk generated considerable interest. This mammoth ivory plaque bears an engraving representing this very same animal, which disappeared from the

In the backdirt of former excavations... *The excavations conducted at La Madeleine, between 1863, the year Lartet and Christy discovered the site, and 1910, when Denis Peyrony intervened on behalf of the State, succeeded in devastating the site. In re-excavating the old backdirt, Peyrony was able to benefit from the "inexperience of the earlier researchers" and salvaged a large limestone slab which bears a splendid carving of a reindeer with a very expressive head.*

region thousands of years ago. The detail of the engraving demonstrates that it was made by a person who was a contemporary of this animal.

The lithic and bone industries from La Madeleine led G. Mortillet to designate this site as the type site for the last period of the Paleolithic. In 1869, he spoke of "the Madeleine Period" and in 1872 he created the term Magdalenian.

Oddly enough, despite its notoriety, the site did not suffer too badly from its early attention and did not receive many visitors. G. Girod, E. Massénat, and E. Rivière undertook excavations here, but fortunately the antiquities dealer, Otto Hauser, believed La Madeleine to be empty and took no interest in the site. This explains why Denis Peyrony was able to conduct methodical excavations from 1910 until the first World War.

This excavation enabled him to distinguish subdivisions in the filling which until then was considered to represent but a single period. The discovery of three, distinct, superposed layers gave rise to a study of the various lithic and bone implements, which defined the types were characteristic of each layer.

This information was immediately put to use by Breuil who at the time was defining the major divisions in the Upper Paleolithic. The defined layers at La Madeleine characterized the last three phases of the Magdalenian (IV, V, VI), while the three preceding phases had been defined earlier at Le Placard in Charente.

Before the monograph on the site was published in 1928, Denis Peyrony undertook a small control excavation in 1926, at which point his good fortune led to the discovery of the burial of a child in the lower level.

The site was abandoned for several decades and left to the pillages of clandestine excavators. Fortunately, these untrained excavators returned thousands of times to go through the same backdirt from previous excavations which still contained a wealth of artifacts. Formal excavations were not reopened until 1968 under the direction of J.-M. Bouvier. These last excavations defined the stratigraphy and included a number of analyses and carbon 14 dating.

The animal species found at La Madeleine give some indication of the food preferences of the prehistoric populations, but they do not represent all of the existing fauna of the period, in that they correspond only to animals that were hunted and eaten. At La Madeleine, one notes a particular dietary preference for reindeer which, in every layer save one, represent 87-100% of the faunal remains. One layer, Magdalenian IV, contains only 63% reindeer, while horse make up 36% of the remains. It appears that other species including ibexes, bison, oxen, chamois, and roedeer make up a very small percentage of the Magdalenians' diet. Note that reindeer were not only a source of food, but also provided skins to make tents, bedding, and clothing, as well as bones and antlers to make needles, awls, bone points or harpoons.

Last but not least, La Madeleine was also an important site for prehistoric art. Hundreds of engraved or sculpted objects originated here. They ranged from the modest to the most spectacular which unfortunately were often removed from the Périgord to national or foreign museums.

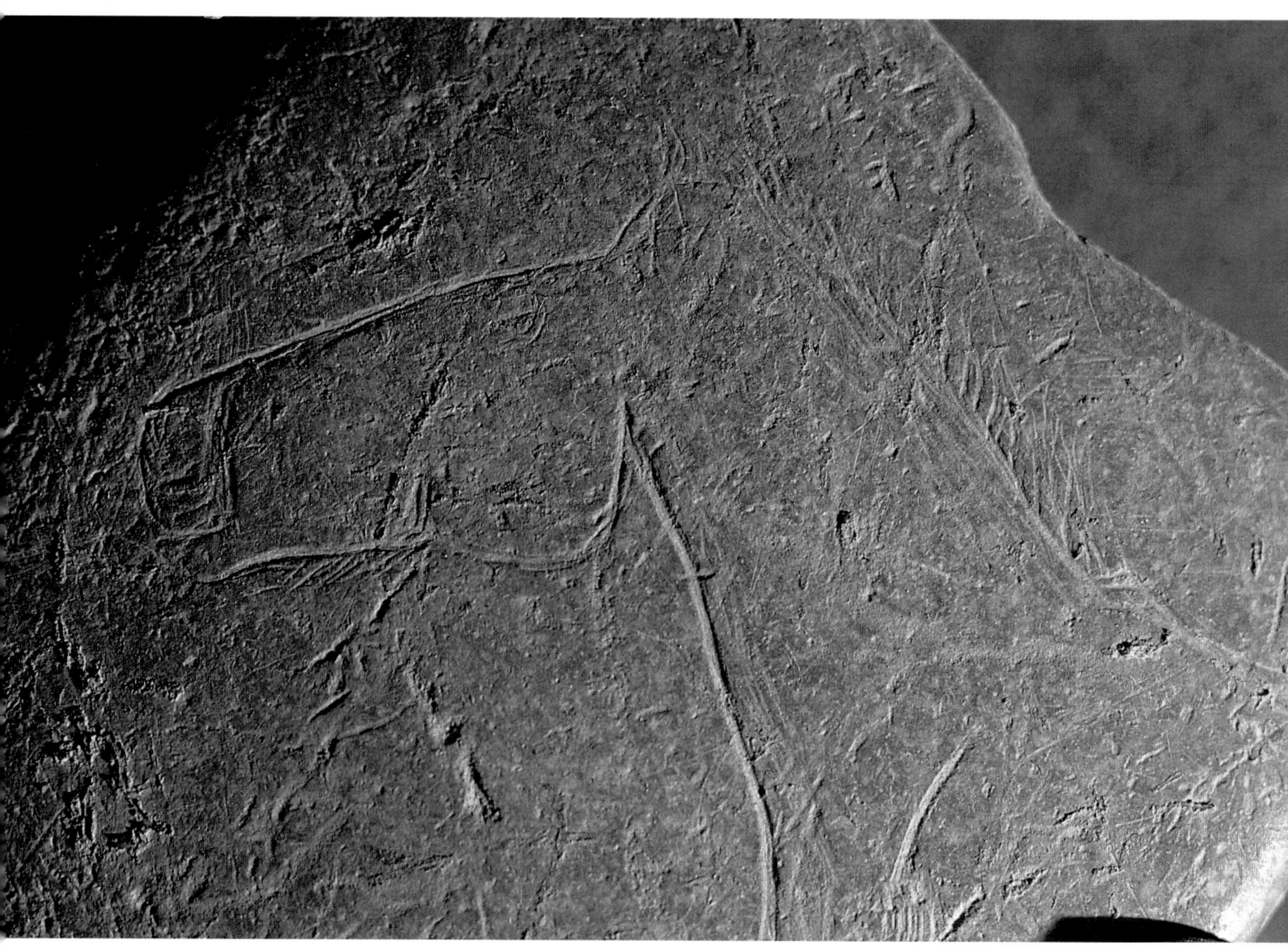

The Magdalenian of Villepin. *The site of Villepin, near La Madeleine, was first occupied in the Magdalenian VI. Three small pebbles were discovered there, including this one in schist, which was decorated with a fairly realistic horse's head. This pebble also bears some indication that it was once used as to pressure flake or retouch flint tools.*

VILLEPIN

The site bears the landlord's name and is located a few dozen meters downstream from La Madeleine "in a savory and wild area", writes Peyrony, who discovered the site and excavated it in 1917. Villepin is also a rock-shelter, though partly collapsed, and is separate from La Madeleine.

Two layers were dated to the Magdalenian VI containing bilaterally barbed harpoons which make them contemporaneous with the third phase of La Madeleine's occupation. A third and top layer clearly corresponds to an Azilian occupation for which only a few sporadic traces remain at La Madeleine. The Magdalenian of Villepin reveals an evolution in the tool assemblage from the lower to the upper layers. This is most evident in the harpoons whose barbs are more pronounced and sharper in the upper layer.

The decorations on awls, and bone points are identical to those found in La Madeleine, indicating a certain affinity. The pebbles are engraved with animals which are often difficult to identify, save the horse, of which only the head and withers are portrayed.

LAUGERIE-BASSE

The site is exceptional. It is a huge cliff, over 500 meters long, which overlooks the Vézère River sixty meters away. At its base, and still 15 meters above the valley floor, erosion carved out rock-shelters which were inhabited in various prehistoric periods. Later, the houses of the hamlet of Laugerie-Basse were built into one of these shelters, using the rocky face as the fourth wall and the overhang as part of the roof.

Excavations, initiated in 1863, were conducted under the main rock-shelter, then the site of a farm house, barn, and stable.

The spectacular cliffs of Laugerie-Basse. *The site is exceptional. It is located at the base of this high cliff, where one may also find the crystallized cave of Le Grand Roc. Today, the main rock-shelter at Laugerie-Basse, has been gutted of all its archaeological filling, while the Abri des Marseilles (above), located under a clutter of stone rubble 50 meters to the right, was only partially excavated.*

The laborers, employed by the prehistorians, dug trenches and even tunneled under buildings in a completely disordered fashion. Lartet and Christy and the Marquis de Vibraye and his associate, Franchet, arrived at the site at the same time, followed closely thereafter by Massénat. Attracted by the phenomenal wealth of the site, especially the works of art, many other prehistorians and amateurs soon followed in what became an uninterrupted parade of visitors for the next fifty years. This onslaught of visitors seriously destroyed the integrity of this site, and a number of artifacts, some of them quite impressive, have neither precise stratigraphic nor chronological provenance.

More serious analyses were not carried out until 1912-1913. This research, conducted by Peyrony and Maury only scratched the surface of the classic shelter. A more in-depth excavation was undertaken under the Abri des Marseilles, located 50 meters upriver, which was to be nearly intact at the time. With the patronage of the famous chemist, Le Bel, Maury was able to dedicate several years to the site's excavation. In 1920, at Le Bel's request, all work was stopped voluntarily, in order to preserve a part of the excavation for future generations.

An analysis of the material unearthed at Laugerie-Basse suggests that the site was occupied from the Magdalenian III to the Magdalenian IV and perhaps also briefly in the Azilian. Vestiges of the Neolithic and of the later Bronze Age were also found in the talus outside the shelter's overhang.

More is known about the occupation of Abri des Marseilles due to the control section which is still visible. The Magdalenians settled on the shelter's natural floor 14,000 years ago. This occupation lasted until the

The woman and the reindeer. *Discovered by Abbé Landesque in 1867 or 1868, this work of art was later acquired by E. Piette. Today, it is preserved at the Musée des Antiquités Nationales. This strange association between a woman and a reindeer was the subject of much discussion. Despite the absence of breasts, the female nature of the human figure is unmistakable, and the volume of the abdomen suggests that this is a woman in a very advanced stage of pregnancy. It is unfortunate that such an unusual piece was found in such a fragmented state.*

Magdalenian VI, when a large section of the overhang suddenly collapsed. Large and thick limestone blocks covered a section of the living site. Nevertheless, the Magdalenians returned and left a few signs of their occupation atop the fallen boulders. The shelter was then abandoned for a long time. Around the year 2,000 B.C., Neolithic people arrived from the Artenac culture. A layer of ash and charcoal were dated to this period, which covered the entire excavated surface of the rock-shelter. The distribution of this combustion debris over such a vast space still cannot be explained. This occupation was followed by further disintegration of the cliff face which left an impressive pile of boulders eight to ten meters high.

Laugerie-Basse's acclaim stems essentially from its wealth in Magdalenian art. The "immodest venus", "the Woman and the Reindeer", and many others are quite famous. All of these pieces are now dispersed across the globe, many of them at the Musée des Antiquités Nationales, the Musée de l'Homme and the British Museum.

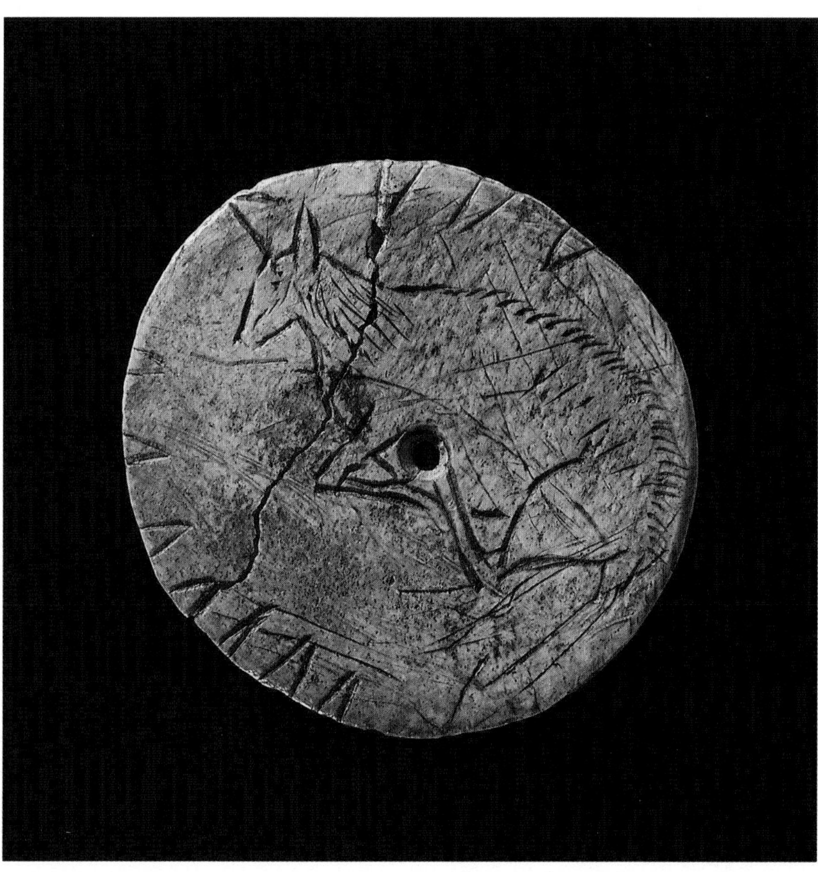

***The chamois disk.** Perforated bone disks, usually cut from the scapulae of herbivores, have been found in several sites and often date to the Magdalenian IV. This intact disk originated at Laugerie-Basse and is now preserved at the Musée du Périgord. Each side bears the portrait of an herbivore, one standing, one resting. Several authors have maintained that they see a chamois on one side associated with a hind on the other.*

RAYMONDEN

Our Magdalenian itinerary now leaves the Vézère Valley to travel further north to the Isle valley and its small tributary, the Beauronne. Four or five kilometers from Périgueux, slightly upstream from Chancelade and its Romanic monastery, an eight hundred meter stretch of cliffs was intensively quarried for cut stone. The small prehistoric cave-site of Raymonden is located by the side of the road, between two rock quarries. Several centuries ago, at this site, an embankment of limestone at cave level was quarried and used to build the grinding stones of a large mill. Some vestiges of this activity are still visible.

The prehistoric site was discovered in March 1876 by M. Hardy, then a correspondent for the "Ministère de l'instruction publique", Ministry of Education, and future archivist and conservator for the Musée du Périgueux.

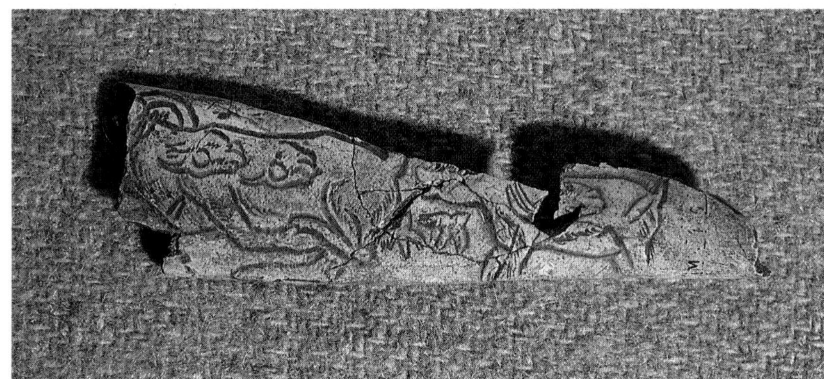

***Fluttering birds.** These small birds seem to have been captured in mid-flight, between two ibexes travelling in single file. When the object is inverted, one can discern another ibex and two other heads of young animals, possibly ibexes or bovines.*

The bison plaquette of Raymonden. *This rib fragment from a large herbivore is split along its width. A hole was made on the left end. The head of a bison, two isolated limbs, and seven small human silhouettes are featured in a puzzling scene. The barbed line behind the bison's head is also a mystery; it is difficult to interpret it as the animal's vertebral column. One of the human figures carries a forked stick. This type of association between a bison and stylized humans is also found on another engraved bone from the site of Château des Eyzies which also dates to the Upper Magdalenian.*

He excavated Raymonden for a while and was succeeded in 1883 by two High School teachers. The site was then left idle until 1887, when the Department built a small railroad line from Périgueux to Brantôme. Ballast was needed, and the talus of Raymonden fit the bill. Laborers dug into the archaeological strata and spread bone and worked flint along nearly three kilometers of tracks, we are told. When the extent of the damage was realized, M. Hardy and M. Féaux decided to conduct a methodical excavation lasting from October 1887 to October 1888. The high point of the dig was a rare discovery of a human burial.

In his monograph, published in 1891, Hardy divided the 1.35 meter-thick "archaeological layer" into four "living floors", each separated by thin layers of sandy or clay soils, which was quite praiseworthy work for this period. The bone or flint tools, faunal remains, and works of art from this site are now preserved at the Musée du Périgord. Unfortunately, no record was made of the provenance of these objects within the stratified deposits. Therefore we have lost invaluable information on the chronological origin of these artifacts. The most we can say, given the presence of certain distinctive materials, is that the entire collection corresponds to the period from Magdalenian IV to VI.

The most famous work of art is the "bison plaquette" whose subject is comparable to another plaquette from the same period in Les Eyzies. This plaquette has been the subject of a number of descriptions and interpretations, some of which are quite picturesque and whimsical.

The burial was found at the base of the site. The body had been laid on its left side, in a tightly flexed position, with the left hand under the head and the right hand under the chin. As was often the case in the Upper Paleolithic, the body had been sprinkled with iron oxide which gave the bones a reddish tint.

Anatomist L. Testut studied the remains and determined that they constituted a particular fossil type or *Homo sapiens* race that differed from Cro-Magnon and Grimaldi: the Chancelade race. This race was rather small (approximately 1.6 meters tall), with elongated crania, high and flat foreheads, and high, broad faces. Chancelade hominids were once compared to the Inuits of Labrador and Greenland whose tool assemblages and lifestyles in similar climatic conditions were somewhat analogous.

Today, such comparisons and associations are no longer considered valid, and even the notion of "race" has been dropped. Instead, irregularities in the fossil record of *Homo sapiens* are attributed to individual variation, sexual dimorphism or discrete evolutionary diversity.

In 1927, L. Didon, a hotel manager in Périgueux and an amateur prehistorian, undertook excavations prior to and immediately after the excavations of Féaux and Hardy. Following his death, J. Bouyssonie succeeded him from 1928 to 1929. The four layers excavated corresponded to the first three stages of the Magdalenian. Thus, had earlier excavations preserved the upper layers, Raymonden would have been the sole site in which a study of the six continuous cultural deposits from the Magdalenian might have been possible. The site itself was excavated too early. But then, might the same not be said for sites currently being excavated?

A strange animal (Musée de Brantôme). *One would be hard pressed to identify the species of this long necked animal with a strange head portrayed above a small engraved motif. Could it be an awkwardly drawn tufted bird or an imaginary animal?*

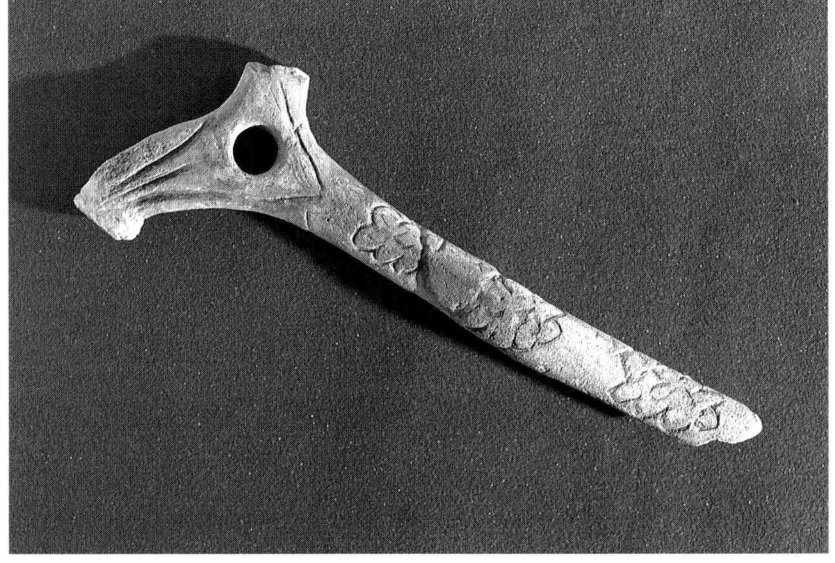

Perforated and decorated baton. *Located close to Rochereil, La Peyzie has yielded several decorated objects from the Upper Magdalenian. This perforated baton, made from reindeer antler, bears a puzzling engraved pattern. Could it be a plant motif?*

ROCHEREIL

We now move on to the Dronne Valley, upstream from the small town of Lisle. The site is adjacent to the Rochereil mill, in a small ten meter square cavity and extends onto a larger terrace in front. Féaux and the Marquis de Fayolle conducted the first excavation here at the turn of the century an excavation which almost cost the life of one of them in a rock fall. However from 1935 to 1939, the best excavations were carried out by P.-E. Jude who went on to publish his findings in 1960.

Two cultural assemblages were identified in the stratigraphy and each was subdivided into several levels. One belongs to the Magdalenian VI well defined by its lithic and bone industry including numerous parrot-beaked burins, Laugerie-Basse points, Teyjat points, bilaterally barbed harpoons, and works of art in a style typical of this phase in the Magdalenian.

The second level was Azilian and contained a rich assemblage of points typical of this period along with flat harpoons made from deer antler. One human burial and the burnt remains of two adolescents were also unearthed and belong to a period we explore further on.

The last bison. *The Teyjat engravings were incised on the smooth surface of amber-colored calcite. The nature of the surface allowed for fine detail in the drawing. This bison, which is otherwise very realistic, has certain anomalies. Due to the clumsiness of the artist, an alteration was made in the lines of the head which made it seem doubled as in a blurred photograph.*

TEYJAT

The Bandiat valley, in which Teyjat is located, is not confined to the Périgord region. The valley passes through parts of Abjat, on the border of the Departments of the Dordogne and Haute-Vienne; it then drops into Nontron and climbs northwest to enter the Charente. Its path outlines almost the entire area of the crystalline outcrops which occupies a small region of the Department's northern territory. At Teyjat, the Bandiat Valley is still in limestone country, a zone highly valued by Paleolithic peoples for its rock-shelters and caves.

The grotte de la Mairie is on the outskirts of the village, near the grade school and the municipal office. Two caves split off from a common entrance. The small gallery is forty meters long, while the long gallery, which is of interest here, is some seventy-five meters long, though the Magdalenian zone does not extend farther than the first fifteen meters.

The prehistoric entrance to the site was discovered in 1889 by Perrier du Carne, and though his published study on Teyjat was subtitled "Magdalenian engravings", it was based on the engravings he found on bones and not the wall engravings discovered in 1903. Perrier du Carne's excavation of the site was somewhat limited but productive. In addition to barbed harpoons, he found five art objects, including one representation of a pony-like horse, engraved on an unusual medium - a reindeer sacrum.

Perrier du Carne made one observation that is very surprising. He stated that within a block of dirt removed with a blow from a pick, he found an imprint in the form of a 1.35 meter-long bow which was still filled with the remains of decomposed wood. Its form was fairly comparable to the well- preserved bows of the Danish Mesolithic. If the bow at la Mairie is indeed from the Magdalenian, it remains the only evidence of it is use in this period.

In 1903, on the advice of Breuil and Cartailhac, Denis Peyrony traveled to Teyjat to see whether the cave contained wall engravings like those he had found in the Les Eyzies region. Indeed, it did. The engravings were made on a calcite film which covered stalagmite formations. Some were in place, others were on fragmented blocks.

The excavations conducted in 1904 by P. Bourrinet, a grade school teacher in Teyjat, led to new discoveries and a detailed study of the living site which extended about fifteen meters from entrance into the cave. Bourrinet's detailed observations, under the supervision of Peyrony and Breuil, revealed two distinct layers separated by a sterile layer of rubble. The oldest layer dates to the Magdalenian V which is characterized by unilaterally barbed harpoons. The upper layer is from the Magdalenian VI with bilaterally barbed harpoons, parrot-beaked burins, and stemmed flint points, later known as Teyjat points.

Several portable art objects were also unearthed at this site. On very surprising piece was an eagle radius upon which a herd of reindeer was portrayed. The first three heads were complete, the thirteen or fourteen that followed were represented by their antlers and oblique hatched lines formed a continuous band at the body level. The head of the last reindeer to close the ranks is also complete.

The surfaces of the limestone walls in the cave are not suitable for engraving. The Magdalenians therefore made use of formations of amber calcite to engrave their images. Parts of the calcite were fractured by falling rubble, and today the engravings are found on slabs of stone, some lying flat, others resting vertically in the archaeological matrix of the Magdalenian V matrix. It is possible that these engravings date to this first period of occupation. This is one of

A photographic realism. *The end of the Magdalenian is marked by a drawing style with a photograph-like realism. This engraving of a cow at Teyjat illustrates the very realistic proportions and posture. It is immediately followed by an aurochs male whose snout is visible here.*

the rare cases in which wall art can be dated directly, since it was found in an archaeological layer.

These engravings form two distinct groups. All the images of the group furthest from the entrance can be clustered together. They form a semicircular composition which begins at the base with a horse turned to the right, above which three aurochs - one male between two females - walk to the left. Higher still near the top of the calcite, a succession of red deer, reindeer, horses, two bison, and a bear are depicted facing in different directions. The images of a second group are more difficult to cluster. This group also associates red deer, a reposed reindeer, a fawn, horses, and a bear.

Forty-eight animals in all were counted at Teyjat including 5 unidentified deer species, 11 red deer, 13 reindeer, 10 horses, 3 aurochs, 4 bison, and 2 portrayed which is an unusual proportion in cave art where horses (Lascaux and Les Combarelles), bison (Font de Gaume), and on rare occasions mammoths (Rouffignac and Bernifal) generally dominate. The number of reindeer (over a quarter of the images) is also unusually high.

The finely incised engravings are of a particular style characterized by a photograph-like realism in the animal's general behavior, proportions, and details. Along with the slightly more recent engravings at Limeuil, they help define the standards of an artistic style - the recent style IV according to A. Leroi-Gourhan - which marks the end of the Magdalenian.

The last hunters of the Vézère. *At Limeuil, the Vézère flows into the Dordogne. This was once the living site of the last great hunters of the reindeer age. Their campsites are now covered by the houses of a medieval village. More than a hundred slabs, plaques and plaquettes were uncovered bearing the engraved images of reindeer, horses, red deer, ibexes, aurochs, and bears. Some believe that Limeuil was once the site of a veritable "atelier".*

This horse is characteristic of Limeuil engravings which date to the Magdalenian VI. This drawing has an almost academic realism which is very different from Lascaux, five thousand years earlier.

The end of the reindeer age. *At Limeuil, reindeer were the most frequently represented animals, whereas previously they were either relatively scarce in number on the walls of caves (Font de Gaume and Les Combarelles) or absent (Rouffignac).*

LIMEUIL

No visible trace of Limeuil's prehistoric occupation remains, because the site, which was excavated at the start of the century, extends beneath the houses, gardens, and streets of the small town, in front of a limestone outcrop which overlooks the confluence of the Vézère and Dordogne Rivers.

Credit for the discovery of the site goes to a retired colonial doctor who uncovered the site, while ground work was being conducted at the home of the village baker, Léo Bélanger. The excavation was conducted from 1909 to 1913 by prehistorian J. Bouyssonie from Brive, who was mandated and financed by "La Direction des Beaux Art", currently the French Ministry of Culture. The excavation was quite arduous and had to proceed using test pits, trenches, and underground tunnels to follow the archaeological strata, in order to respect the structures overhead.

The excavated site extended for a thirty meters along the base of a slope below two outcrops of limestone and constituted an open air site with the use of a small cliff overhang upslope.

The strata date to the Magdalenian VI and are characterized by an overabundance of parrot-beaked burins and bilaterally barbed harpoons. The engravings on bone and reindeer antler are characteristic of the period. Other objects included a beautiful perforated baton decorated with fishes and macrocephalic reindeer, and other pieces featuring bison, horses and even a fox, a species rarely depicted in prehistoric art.

The novelty of this site of Limeuil is the abundance of engraved limestone plaquettes, plaques and blocks. Bouyssonie published descriptions of

Headless women. *The last Magdalenians, who drew very realistic animals, sometimes also made very simplified female profiles which consisted of torsos and backsides without heads, arms, or legs. Several Lalinde blocks could not be placed stratigraphically until the discovery of another block bearing this female representation under the nearby rock-shelter of Gare de Couze. Observations made by Professor Bordes, who excavated the site, allowed for exact dates to be attributed to these objects which are Magdalenian VI in age.*

over a hundred documents. Limeuil was seen by him as the site of a prehistoric art workshop, and he compared its art objects to the pages of a sketchbook. Some are rough sketches which are often jumbled together, others works are more detailed, and still others are true master pieces.

This very romantic explanation does not stem from a very rigorous scientific analysis which might otherwise eliminate some of its more imaginative aspects. However, it would be difficult to replace this interpretation with another that could explain a site so rich in engraved stones of all sizes which seem to have been discarded along side flaked flint tools and food remains. It is difficult to imagine Limeuil as a sanctuary composed of portable art.

What is certain is that these pieces are of a rare quality and display a marked stylistic homogeneity. As in Teyjat, we find representations with photograph-like realism in anatomical details, proportions, and behavior: a lowered head of a grazing reindeer, rutting reindeer, a herd of red deer in which one has its head raised on the alert, galloping horses, etc. On several occasions, a line drawn at the animals' feet seems to indicate the ground level which is rarely depicted in Paleolithic art.

And like Teyjat, red deer and reindeer are the most common and constitute half of the animals represented, followed by horses (a third), oxen, bison, and ibexes. Two bears were also present. Other species are also represented but their publications must await completion of an ongoing critical examination of the entire sample of engravings.

Thus it is here, where the Vézère flows into the Dordogne, that we come to the end of this prestigious tour of the Magdalenian. This royal tour of prehistory took us from Lascaux to Limeuil, and in a distance of thirty kilometers, covered more than five thousand years time.

6. The Mesolithic and Neolithic. From 9,500 to 3,000 B.C.

A Climatic Crisis (or Farewell to the Reindeer)

The golden age of reindeer hunters, an age of abundance in which the prehistoric occupants of the Périgord had the free time to develop the magnificent cave and rock-shelter art, slowly faded away. The icy winters of glacial times were followed by periods of climatic instability; phases of humid and relatively temperate climates intermixed with periods of bitter cold, but the general trend was one of gradual warming.

What caused these climatic changes? An answer is only now emerging and astronomy holds key. They were not caused by a shift in the poles as was once believed, but rather a difference in the tilt of the earth's axis. While the difference was only slight, it was enough to bring on shorter winters and longer days. 9,000 years ago, summer was nine days shorter and the winter seven and a half days longer than it is today. A few extra minutes of sunshine and fewer days of winter were enough for the countryside to become progressively unrecognizable. In the Périgord, as well as nearly all over Europe, the progressive changes that culminated over dozens or hundreds of years must have had significant if not dramatic consequences for the lives of prehistoric people. Locally, the poorly understood weather systems, position of anticyclones, wind conditions, and the flow of ocean currents probably played a significant role.

Around 9,500-9,000 B.C., due to a relatively temperate oscillation, the reindeer began to leave the Périgord which no longer provided its usual food source - lichen. The countryside was already no longer a steppe with sparse tree cover that was once the home of Magdalenian hunters. Humidity favored the growth of deciduous trees. The once open terrain was darkened and with it the lives of the Périgord inhabitants. The world "they" knew was disintegrating. Their favorite game became scarce, and rain flooded their camps. One last rigorous cold period hinted that the good times would return, but alas, the glacial times were gone forever. The reindeer would no longer return nor would the many animals frequently featured in cave paintings. The time of forest animals had arrived. These included red deer, boar, roe deer, and less remarkable small game, which were more difficult to hunt because they did not live in large herds but rather alone or in small groups. The traditional hunts and the good times were no more !

The last reindeer were hunted 11 to 12,000 years ago in the Dordogne valley at Couze and in the Morin rock-shelter near Pessac-sur-Dordogne (which today is located in Gironde, near its border with the Périgord). Did they take refuge in the cooler regions of the Pyrenees or the Grands Massifs in the warm summer months like the ibex? Or were they able to travel north and reach the latitudes at which reindeer live today? Whatever the case may be, contrary to an all too popular belief, the Magdalenians did not follow the reindeer into northern regions. Their direct descendants the Azilians, remained in the country where their abilities to adapt were put to the test, until a new lifestyle could be developed.

These adaptations were gradual like the changes themselves. In the still sparse forests, a spear propelled by a hooked atlatl was still equally effective in hunting red deer or boar as it had been in hunting reindeer. The flint points which armed these spears - Azilian points - hardly changed. These had steeply retouched

Azilian flints from the Abri de Villepin (Tursac). *The Azilian flint points, identical to points from the final Magdalenian, were used as spearpoints. Other tools like the short end-scraper, truncated blade, and the burin were used in daily activities to work hides and bone, and cut wood.*

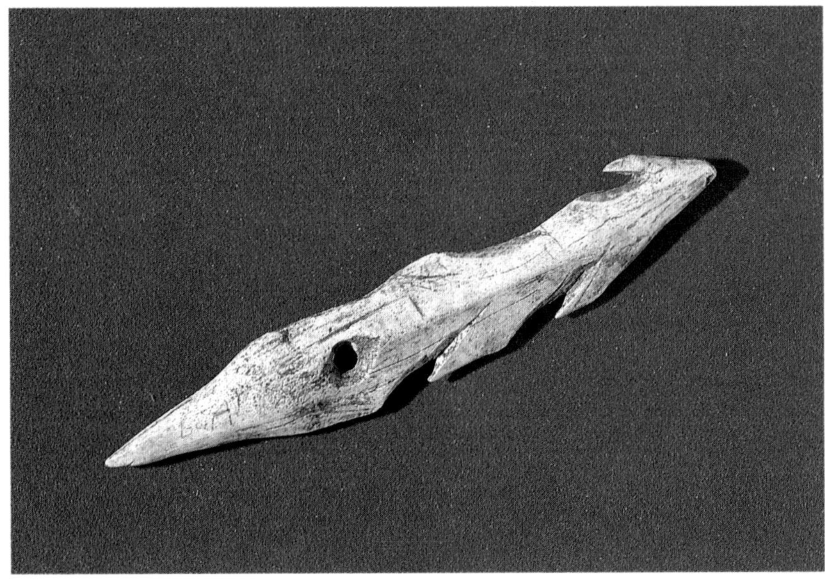

Azilian harpoon with a perforated base from Rochereil (Musée de Brantôme). *The flat Azilian harpoons are not as impressive as the Magdalenian harpoons, but the spongy nature of the material did not allow for anything better. It is questionable as to whether harpoons were used for fishing. They may have served in the hunt or even been suspended as hooks.*

backs, and had previously armed the tips of Magdalenian spears. All Azilian tool assemblages were clearly derived from the preceding period. The changes were relatively minor and consisted of smaller, more numerous end-scrapers and a more limited quantity of burins. However, the great tradition of tools made from reindeer antler was lost with the disappearance of the reindeer itself.

Were these the products of a more precarious lifestyle? The caves and rock-shelters no longer seem to have been a source of inspiration for the prehistoric painters or engravers. Azilian artists preferred to paint or engrave stone or bone plaquettes, and pebbles, as if they had an aversion consecrating stationary sanctuaries. These were the last expressions of a naturalist art. The engravings of horses or bovids displayed a very different style from the Magdalenian, even from the preceding Magdalenian VI. However, when we examine the series of lines engraved on limestone pebbles, like the one from Rochereil, we can no longer decipher the message Azilian artists are

A strange horse. *This engraving comes from the Azilian period at Pont d'Ambon and is one of the rare figurative engravings known from this period. Its style is original and unrelated to that of the Magdalenian. The head and limbs are filled with hatched lines and the outline is accented by tiny criss-crosses and extremely fine incisions. The animal's proportions are surprising. The head is abnormally long and the legs are dwarfed.*

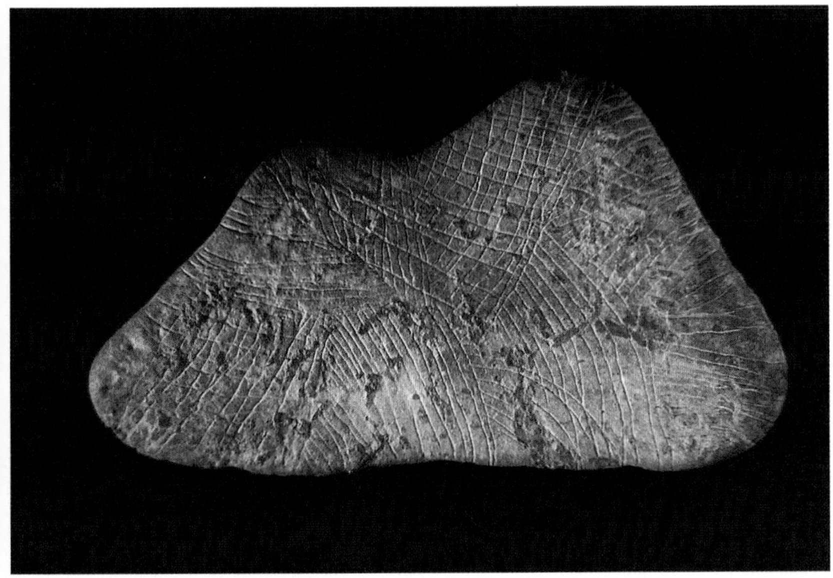

The engraved pebble of Rochereil. *This small six centimeter long limestone pebble, coated with ochre, is decorated on one side with fine regular incisions organized into ten separate sections. What could be the meaning hidden behind these complex motifs? Magic? Sorcery?*

attempting to relay, unless, they knowingly and deliberately hid the message in their graphic designs.

The descendants of reindeer hunters, who learned to hunt deer and boar, were fortunate that fishing was an option, since the aquatic life was less directly affected by the climatic changes. As the Magdalenians before them, some Azilian campsites, like Rochereil and Pont d'Ambon, or La Madeleine and Villepin were located at the edge of the Dronne and Vézère Rivers respectively. The abundance of fish at Pont d'Ambon practically makes it a specialized site. The reoccupation of the old Magdalenian sites is a sign of continuity even though temporary open air camps were established elsewhere.

The only known skeletal remains of Périgord Azilians are those of a medium sized male (1.6 meters high) from Rochereil with traits similar to the ''Chancelade race'', and two individuals -one male one female - from Peyrat at Saint-Rabier near Terrasson. In the latter case, the male is 1.67 meters high and the female only 1.56 meters. The man's face is rather broad. The woman's skull is missing.

Mesolithic habitat from the porch of Rouffignac cave. *Between 9,200 and 7,800 years ago, Mesolithic hunters occupied the porch area of Rouffignac cave, where several superposed hearths, abundant animal bones, and worked flint - especially geometric microliths from the Sauveterrian - were uncovered. The upper levels contained burials from the Neolithic and the metal age.*

THE MESOLITHIC AND EARLY NEOLITHIC: FROM THE WOODS TO OPEN CLEARINGS

The Mesolithic culture: forest hunters

Around 8,000 B.C., the climate was still dry and cold, but not glacial. Conditions gradually became milder over time. Norwegian pine and birch tree progressively lost ground. In the mid 7th millennium B.C., hazel and oak forests began to obscure the Périgord's horizon. Gradually, a large pristine forest emerged, with game animals, fur-bearers, and dangerous carnivores like bears and wolves.

Humans developed the bow and arrow for survival and self-defence. The bow, one of the first man made machines, may have originated in the Upper Paleolithic, but the great post-glacial hunters, the forest dwellers, adopted it as their weapon of choice. The bows from some bogs from Northern Europe, made from yew tree, give some idea of the lost bows from the Périgord's Mesolithic. The arrow is a precision weapon, superior to the spear, and very deadly with speeds exceeding one hundred kilometers an hour. However these single curved bows could have drawn only the lightest projectiles. Thus, prehistoric hunters armed their arrows with miniature flint points. The smallest points were only a few millimeters long and weighed less than a gram. They must have been mounted on reed stalks using resin, fish or other animal glues. Sometimes traces of these adhesives can be discerned on these minuscule worked flints, or "microliths", micropoints or geometric pieces like triangles, lunates, and trapezoids.

The life of hunters was not sedentary. They travelled across their hunting and fishing territories, fully exploited seasonal resources, and partook of fruits, seeds, and wildberries along the way like all forest dwellers. Open air camps are still largely unknown in the Périgord. The chosen habitats were rock-shelters or cave entrances like Contie cave at Coulaures in the Isle basin, and especially Rouffignac cave in the Vézère basin. For over a thousand years, hunters returned here to camp, knap flint (whose nodules piled up against the cave walls), and light fires around which they planted stakes to hold spits to roast boar or red deer unted in the area.

They abandoned tiny flints characteristic of the Sauveterrian culture named after the type site Sauveterre-la-Lémance located in the historic (although not administrative) Périgord region. It is known that microliths, minuscule triangles, sharpened bipoints (Sauveterrian points), points with truncated bases (Rouffignac points), were made in situ, since we find microburins and flint knapping debitage associated with them. Larger tools such as end-scrapers, and especially denticulates, are attributed to other activities like working wood. Flint knives have a unique polish that usually stems from cutting silicious plants. However, it is unlikely that these plants were grain stalks, since wild grains were present only in the Near East, and cereal agriculture did not appear in the West until later in the Neolithic. The inhabitants of Rouffignac probably harvested plants for bedding or baskets.

Had the dog already been domesticated? It is quite possible. Immediately following glacial times, small wolves appear that were either in the process of domestication or already domesticated. They may be the predecessors to our dogs. In any case, dogs did accompany the last Mesolithics at Rouffignac 8,000 years ago.

It is unclear what Périgord Mesolithic peoples looked like. Unfortunately, a skull, believed to be from the Sauveterrian, from Roc du Barbeau (Musée des Eyzies) has disappeared.

The First Step Toward a Farming Culture

6,000 or 7,000 years ago, significant changes occurred which had already been for a long time in the eastern part of the Mediterranean basin. A new lifestyle gradually changed the hunters of the forest into the first agriculturalists. What prompted this first spark? What transformed these last hunters into the first farmers and shepherds? The first signs appear a thousand years earlier with a change in the tool assemblage. Little by little, trapezoids replace the triangular flints, and microliths become larger. By the mid 5th millennium, true "tranchet"' arrow-points, generally triangular with invasive retouch, appear in the upper levels of the Mesolithic at Rouffignac, Roc du Barbeau, and Peyrat near Saint-Rabier. At Rouffignac, the level is believed to date to 6,400 years ago, based on carbon 14 dating. These tiny arrow heads and the first microliths with invasive retouch which accompany them are found throughout southern France. They belonged to the first herders and farmers of the Neolithic.

THE STONE AXE FARMERS

The Polished Stone Culture

The new dawn for humanity was marked by the emergence of a rural economy based on animal husbandry and plant cultivation. Efficient tools were needed to cut down trees, open clearings in the forest, turn up the fertile top soil, sow precious seeds, protect the crops from trampling, and harvest and store the grains. In the beginning, Neolithic farmers continued to use the tools inherited from their Mesolithic predecessors, but they soon invented new ones. For the heavy work like cutting trees and breaking the top soil, as well as other more delicate tasks, the polished axe became the basic Neolithic tool. Rich in flint and hard cobblestones, the Périgord was an excellent source of raw materials. Thus, for example, the grey-green dolerite pebbles that from the Limousin, were rolled by the Auvézère and the Isle River to be deposited just downstream from Périgueux. These were ultimately transformed into polished (or ground) stone axes. By 6,000 years ago, the excellent flint deposits at Bergerac supplied axe production workshops which lasted at least 2,000 years.

Middle Neolithic Burials in Caves and Dolmens

When these workshops appeared, approximately 5,000 years ago, farming and animal breeding communities were already settled in the Périgord region. Their villages, which are still not well known, must have been perched on rocky spurs where the natural erosion and millenia of agriculture erased any trace.

Flaked flint axes from Bergerac (Musée d'Aquitaine). *Neolithic people made extensive use of the excellent flint of the Bergerac region. Here, one finds flint knapping workshops for the production of axes. Some delicately flaked axes, ready for polishing, were true masterpieces. Indeed, they were sometimes used as is.*

Polishing stone from Les Justices near Mauzens-Miremont. *The flaked stone axes were polished against blocks of sandstone with the aid of an abrasive made of wet sand. This grindstone bears grooves for the sharp edges of axes and depressions for the flat sides. It may have taken ten hours or so to produce a finished polished axe.*

Laugerie-Haute, the Abri du Squelette. *This rock-shelter yielded at least three skeletons discovered accidentally in 1938, while dynamiting the shelter s large fallen blocks. The bones belong to a man more than 60 years old and another man, 25 to 30 years old. It was not possible to study the third. Some characteristics, including a long cranium, a fairly wide face and nose, and low orbits, seem to link them to the Upper Paleolithic or Mesolithic populations. An Early or Middle Neolithic vase was found in close proximity.*

Grotte de Campniac in Coulounieix-Chamiers. *Campniac opens into the vallon of Vieille-Cité near Périgueux. It yielded human bones sometimes burned as well as polished axes, flaked flint implements, bone tools, and ornaments. The human remains could be those of the inhabitants of the Ecorneboeuf hillsite which overlooks the valley.*

Others settled lower in the valleys and are possibly still buried in the alluvial deposits. Among the rock-shelters or caves that were occupied in this period, the Neolithic deposits were often destroyed by earlier excavators in search of... paleolithic remains. This is certainly the case of the famous sites around Les Eyzies, such as Laugerie-Basse, Laugerie-Haute, La Mouthe, among others.

Middle Neolithic vessel from Grotte de Campniac (Musée du Périgord). *Campniac was occupied in the Middle, Late and Final Neolithic. This round-based vase comes from the Middle Neolithic, as do several "tranchet" arrowheads, polished axe heads, and ornaments deposited in the cave.*

The Blanc dolmen at Nojals-et-Clottes or Cros-de-la-Vuige. *This passage-grave, often incorrectly called "the gallery grave of Blanc at Beaumont", is located on a hill that was probably modified by the Neolithics. Its present state does not reflect the original architecture. An additional upright flagstone was placed along the length of the chamber. Today one enters from the destroyed back part of the dolmen, while the true entrance was at the opposite end through a now collapsed trilith, characteristic of the so called Angers type (or Loire type).*

The dolmen of Paussac-Saint-Vivien. *In its present state, La Peyrolevado de Paussac is the product of a deplorable restoration that departs completely from the original layout. Only two supports are in their original places. This may be another Anger's type chambered tomb like the Blanc dolmen.*

The Point-du-Jour dolmen (Vergt-de-Biron). *At the border of the Dordogne and Lot-et-Garonne, the Point-du-Jour dolmen rises on a promontory overlooking the Dropt Valley. Its enormous, six meter, reddish, sandstone cap-stone rests on two rows of supports which collapsed under its weight. This is definitely not a gallery grave, but it may be an Angers type dolmen, like the Blanc dolmen, whose entrance structures should have been altered.*

The chambered tombs: house of the dead or monument for the living?

5,000 years ago or possibly slightly earlier, strange monuments made of slabs of raw or roughly worked stone called "dolmens" appeared in the Périgord and in Charente nearby. A few erect stone slabs delineate a polygonal or rectangular chamber which is covered by a large cap-stone. This chamber is preceded by an antechamber of shorter vertical stone slabs or dry stone walling, once covered by capstones. Perhaps, as in neighboring Charente, the Périgord saw the emergence of dolmens entirely built with dry stones like the "bories" of our ancestors. These constructions were usually covered by a burial mound or barrow. Once buried under the mound, the chamber resembles a cave. Unfortunately, time and human activity have altered these monuments. Deprived of their burial mounds, and their gallery, and reduced to a few slanted or collapsed slabs, they are now no more than pathetic ruins.

The wealth of dolmens in the Périgord is still largely undocumented. The one hundred recognized monuments is a respected figure for a French region, but nearly everything was pillaged by treasure hunters who were surely left disappointed. Thus, we often have no idea as to what they once contained, their date of construction, nor their original architecture. They may have been in use for 1,000 years at least, but it is only by comparing them with others in neighboring regions, especially the West, that it is possible to situate them chronologically.

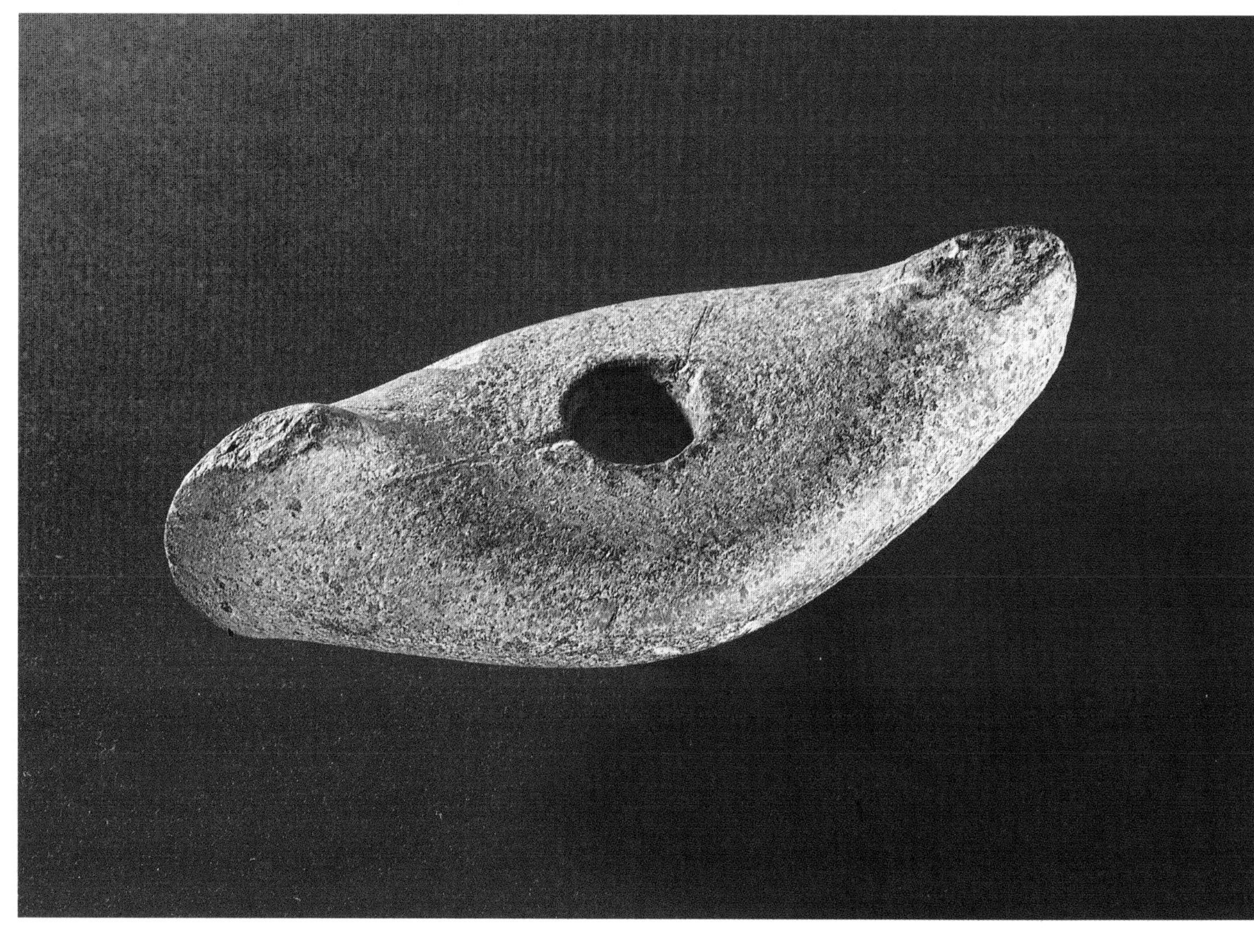

Perforated boat-shaped axe from Saint-Sulpice de Mareuil (private collection). *This boat shaped axe is made from imported stone (hornblendite possibly from Brittany). Similar axes have been found in the Val de Loire. Given their elaborate shape and the softness of the rock from which they are made, they probably had a more symbolic than utilitarian value.*

Late Neolithic causewayed camps and collective cave burials

As the last big dolmens were being erected, the Périgord's countryside continued to change. In the beginning of the third millennium B.C., the Late Neolithic cultures of Charente, Matignons, and Peu-Richard radiated outward to the basins of the Dronne and the Isle. Late Neolithic pottery was of lower quality than those of the Middle Neolithic, and produced only a few fine vases with incised or relief decoration. Flaked or polished stone tools were far more abundant. New implements include axe-hammers, battle-axes, and mace-heads with shaft-holes. Their fabrication was time-consuming and difficult, and the end product was fragile. They were probably not tools but rather weapons or insignias of some high authority. Their symbolic power might have been comparable to the double-edged axe of Aegean civilization. Approximately 4,500 years ago, "battle" axes of this shape in stone (or sometimes in copper) emerged throughout Europe, from Scandinavia and the Ukraine to the Atlantic. To this day, only about thirty axes or fragments of this type have been found in the Périgord.

Like their neighbors in Charente, residents of the Dordogne adopted or developed ditched enclosures. On elevated terrain or even on the plains, ditches were dug to form more or less circular causewayed camps. Aerial photograph revealed ditches one of these in Celles in the northern Périgord. These ditches, which were dug using picks made from a red deer antler or from flint, might also have served as quarries. The extracted raw materials were used to build up the banks, and smaller constructions, which have since been completely destroyed by erosion and centuries of plowing. It is unclear why people dug enclosure ditches in sandy or gravel soils as in the Isle valley (Fontaine de la Demoiselle at Saint-Léon-sur-l'Isle).

The Campniac vase (Musée du Périgord). *A vase shaped like a flower pot with flat bottom and ears. Coarse clay including vegetal temper, awkward modelling skills, and incomplete firing were all characteristics of the late Neolithic pottery.*

Campniac necklace (Musée du Périgord). *This museum reconstituted necklace incorporates elements found separately in the cave, including perforated animal teeth, stone beads and limestone pendants.*

***A general view of Eybral cave at Le Coux-et-Bigaroque.** Opened in the small valley of a tributary of the Dordogne River, it was practically filled with clay and contained a jumble of bones from nearly eighty skeletons of men, women, and children, some of which were burned. This collective burial dates to the Late Neolithic.*

More is known bout the burials of this period than about the settlements. Collective burials, sometime containing several dozen skeletons, were discovered in caves in the Isle basin at Campniac or in the Dordogne basin at Eybral. Often the bones had been moved, arranged and sometimes burned. The grave goods were often quite poor and included a rare polished axe (often made of flint), crude flat-bottomed pottery, perforated animal teeth, limestone beads, buttons with two holes made from bone or the shells of fresh water mussels. The cultural assemblage, associated with these tombs, has come to be called "the Isle-Dordogne group". The same populations may have reused or even built their own dolmens. The gallery graves in the southern Périgord (Marsalès) may date to this period, but they have long since been pillaged of all their contents. Based on several traits in the funerary ritual and the goods associated with the burials, this Isle-Dordogne group in the Périgord seems to closely resemble the Seine-Oise-Marne group from the Late Neolithic in the Paris basin.

***Trepannated skull, Eybral cave.** The skull of a young adult with two healed trepannations, one very large hole (90mm long by 55mm wide) at the crown of the head, the other at the back of the head (50mm by 40mm). There is no sign of infection, which demonstrates the effectiveness of the "surgeons" who operated using flint tools.*

***A frontal section at Fontaine de la Demoiselle, Saint-Léon sur l'Isle** (excavation by Roussot-Larroque). This site was occupied in the Late Neolithic (colour bandings in white sand) and later in the Final Neolithic (reddish brown sand). Interrupted ditches dug into the sands by the first occupants were re-excavated by the Artenacians of the Final Neolithic. Parts of the ditches were refilled by the Artenacians with a mix of potsherds and cobblestones. Why these ditches were dug in a sandy soil remains an unanswered riddle.*

These collective burials have revealed more information about the skeletal morphology of the Périgord populations of 4,700 years ago. In many ways, they resemble their ancestors. It is unlikely that immigrations changed the fundamental characteristics of this population. Their skulls were elongated, sometimes carinated, and their faces were fairly wide, but they were probably generally less robust than Upper Paleolithic populations. Changes in living conditions may account for a great deal. The pressures for selection which were still quite high in the Upper Paleolithic decreased gradually in the Neolithic. A drop in the meat content of the diets of new farmers and increased protection against the elements and other dangers, also meant a far more favorable environment for the sick, the elderly, and children. The gracilization that ensued is clearly visible when one compares Neolithic skeletons to those of the Paleolithic. This process is equivalent to skeletal reductions observed in domesticated animals compared to their wild ancestors. Humans are self-domesticated animals.

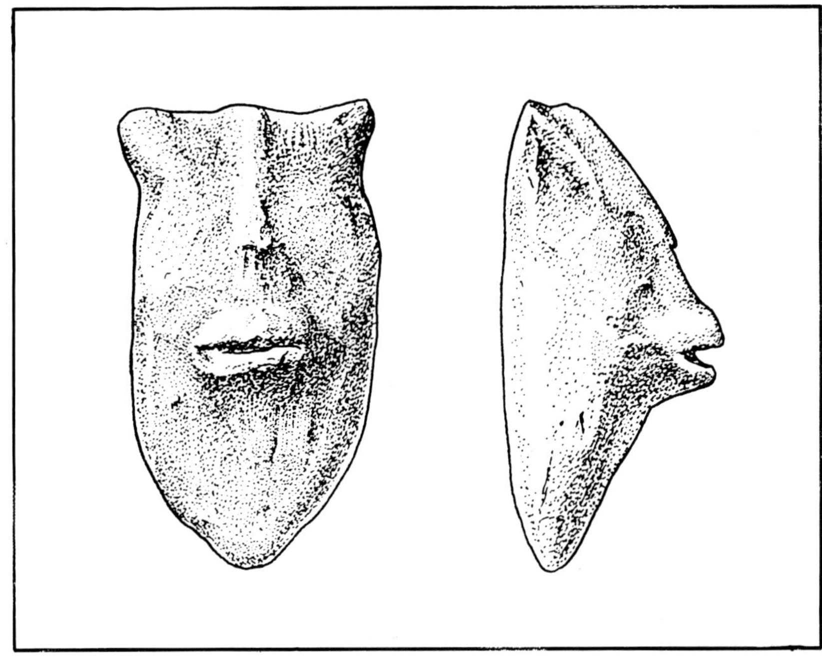

***Baked clay figurine from Les Plaguettes at Razac-de-Saussignac (private collection).** Discovered at a site occupied by the Artenacians, this mask figurine measures six centimeters in length. Its features are anthropomorphic, with a flat nose, lips projecting outward into a mouth, and a pointed chin. Today, this very expressive and strange figurine is the only one of its kind from French Neolithic art (drawing actual size).*

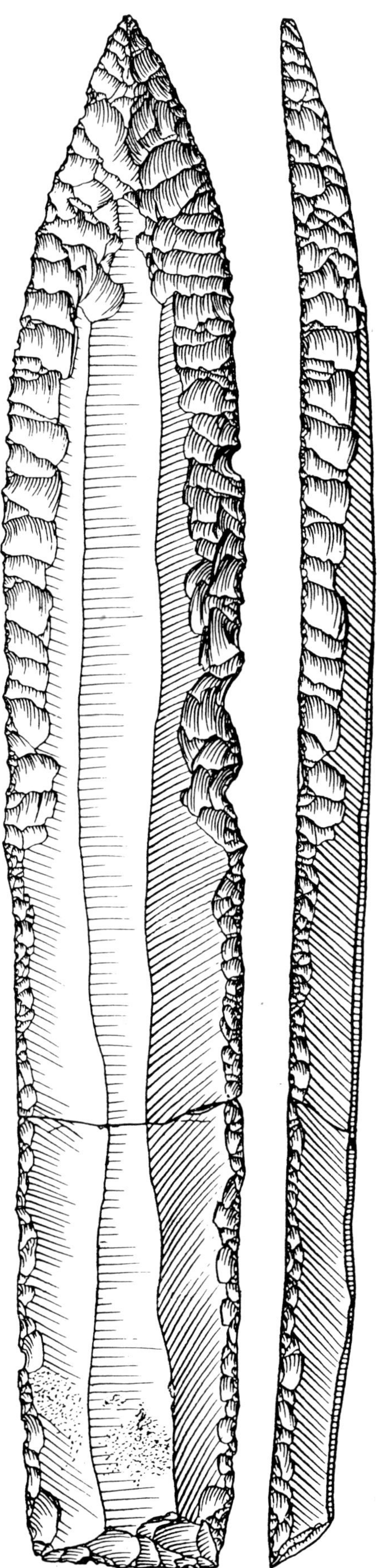

Flint dagger found in the Périgord. *The two parts of this long blade from Chancelade were uncovered eleven years apart. It is over 23 centimeters long and is retouched along the sides and at the point. The blade illustrates the knapping techniques of the Final Neolithic.*

Flint dagger from Saint-Seurin-de-Prats. (private collection). *The dorsal side bears uniform oblique retouch, made after the piece was polished. These daggers were used for peaceful purposes. The most perfectly formed were prestige items. It may also be the case with the flint blades of Grand Pressigny near Tours.*

''Livres de Beurre'' of Lamonzie-Montastruc (private collection). *These Bergerac flint cores were prepared for the flaking of long blades using the technique practiced in Grand Pressigny workshops.*

The Cayrelevat dolmen at Siorac. *This picturesque dolmen, not far from another at Bonarme, is partially collapsed. Polished axes were found around it.*

Changes in the Final Neolithic

The appearance of the first copper objects about 3,000 B.C. did not spell the immediate disappearance of the Neolithic civilization. Perhaps stimulated by competition with the new metal, flint knapping reached new heights with barbed and tanged arrowheads and large retouched blades, or ''knives'', at times exceeding 20 centimeters in length. Flint blades were imported from Grand Pressigny near Tours, knapped from specially prepared cores called ''pounds of butter'' (''livres de beurre''). Flint knappers from Bergerac tried to imitate and export them without a great success. ''Livres de beurre'' have been found near Lanquais and in the Montclar forest.

The Périgord was then in the midst of a very dynamic culture, the Artenacian, which extended from Normandy to Limousin and Quercy. Fine ceramics bore incised or pointillé decorations. The typical handles were beak or nose shaped. The inhabitants lived on promontories, on the edge of plateaux, in valleys, and even at the water's edge. They occupied the Dronne, Isle, Vézère, and Dordogne basins. Near Eternel, the great earthmovers, the Artenacians, dug ditches, built earthen and stone ramparts, and planted wooden posts in marshlands. Cultivators and animal breeders colonized rocky and sandy soils which until then were sparsely occupied lands. Caves, rock-shelters and megaliths served for collective burials. They reused dolmens and built new ones. Though often smaller and simpler than in the Middle Neolithic, these were quite numerous particularly in the Isle basin (Saint-Aquilin) and in southern Périgord (Saint-Pardoux-et-Vielvic).

The Peyre Nègre dolmen near Nojals-et-Clottes. *Not far from the Blanc dolmen, Peyre Nègre in Nojals, with its large cap-stone of brown silicious rock, is one of the most picturesque megaliths in the region.*

The dolmen of Cantegrel at Saint-Chamassy *(see following pages). Partly buried beneath a bank, the Cantegrel dolmen possesses a rectangular chamber. One of the uprights bears the grooved marks of its use as a polishing stone. An excavation conducted in the late 19th century reportedly uncovered a skeleton lying diagonally in this chamber and holding a flint implement in its hand.*

7. From the dawn of copper to the Iron Age: From 3,000 to 700 B.C.

The first metals - gold and copper - had arrived. Neolithic people had an unusual fascination for these metals. But for the production of daily tools, stone was still supreme. Beginning about 3,000 B.C, a progressive but inevitable evolution began in our region with the use of copper daggers and axes. Metallurgy, which appeared much earlier in the Near East and the Balkans, was first introduced to the southern rim of the Massif Central, Cévennes, and Haut-Languedoc which are rich in metal deposits. Possibly a little later, raw materials from Limousin, the Eastern Périgord, and the Pyrenees were discovered and exploited. These copper pyrites and grey coppers were more difficult to reduce than azurite and malachite. In any case, the flat copper axes, which continued to imitate the shape of polished stone axes, were found in the Périgord, either isolated or in small hoards of two or three axes as at Saint-Capraise-d'Eymet and Saint-Martial-d'Artenset. One axe was found in association with the copper daggers of Fontanguillère. These flat tanged daggers extended from Portugal to Scotland, from the Atlantic to Central Europe, and were directly associated with the bell-beakers decorated in zones or parallel horizontal lines using a cord or comb.

The rise of the Early Bronze Age and the first Périgord princes

Several centuries later, it was discovered that alloying tin and copper improved the qualities of the metal: bronze was invented. Since it was not yet understood how to reduce tin ore, a smelt of raw tin oxide, panned from selected waterways, was added to copper. Some of Britanny's streams may have been used for this purpose, and perhaps tin ores were also imported from the northwest of Spain or nearby Limousin (Monts de Blond). As techniques improved, poor quality bronze with a low tin content, advanced to a true bronze with 10% tin or more. The Périgord was influenced by the large waves of innovation which passed through the valleys, especially the Dordogne,

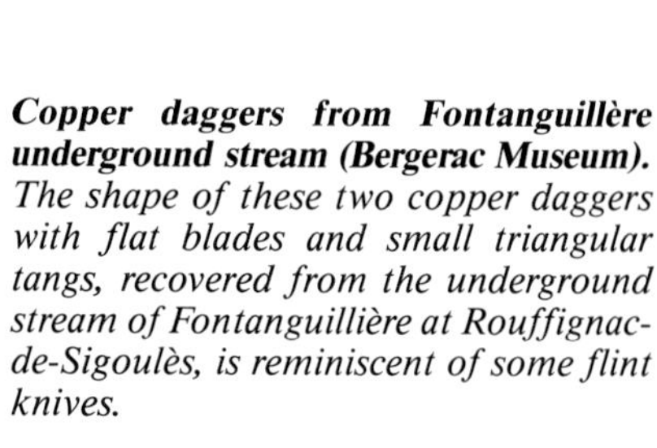

Copper daggers from Fontanguillère underground stream (Bergerac Museum). *The shape of these two copper daggers with flat blades and small triangular tangs, recovered from the underground stream of Fontanguillière at Rouffignac-de-Sigoulès, is reminiscent of some flint knives.*

Flat copper axes from Manzac-sur-Vern and Boulazac (Musée du Périgord) *The first metal axes imitated the shapes of stone axes.*

from the east by the Massif Central. The first low flanged axes, which were perfected from the flat axe, appeared at times with a hammer decoration (Saint-Méard-de-Dronne).

In Port-Sainte-Foy, on the eastern limits of the Gironde, dredging of the Dordogne produced several thin bronze daggers with rivet holes, and a ring-headed pin similar to Swiss and Italian types. A dagger from Coux-et-Bigaroque, also dredged from the Dordogne, bears a pattern of engraved lines and dots, similar to examples from the Rhone Culture, as the bronze hilted knives from Ripatransone in northern Italy. The long dagger from Singleyrac tomb near Bergerac (sometimes attributed to Saint-Aubin-de-Cadelech) evokes the same Rhone civilization. The hollow bronze hilt of this 40 centimeter-long dagger was probably cast in the lost wax process and riveted to the blade. The rich offerings deposited in this stone-walled cist include thirteen gold spirals, a gold ring, a gold rod, and a flat axe. These deposits suggest the existence of a princely caste in the Périgord, contemporary with the "princes" of the Early Bronze Age in Armorique, Wessex, or Saxony. We regret all the more the disappearance of these grave-goods, and the destruction of the skeleton whose skull was said to have been so hard that it survived several swift boot kicks before it was finally shattered beneath the blows of a pick-axe (!).

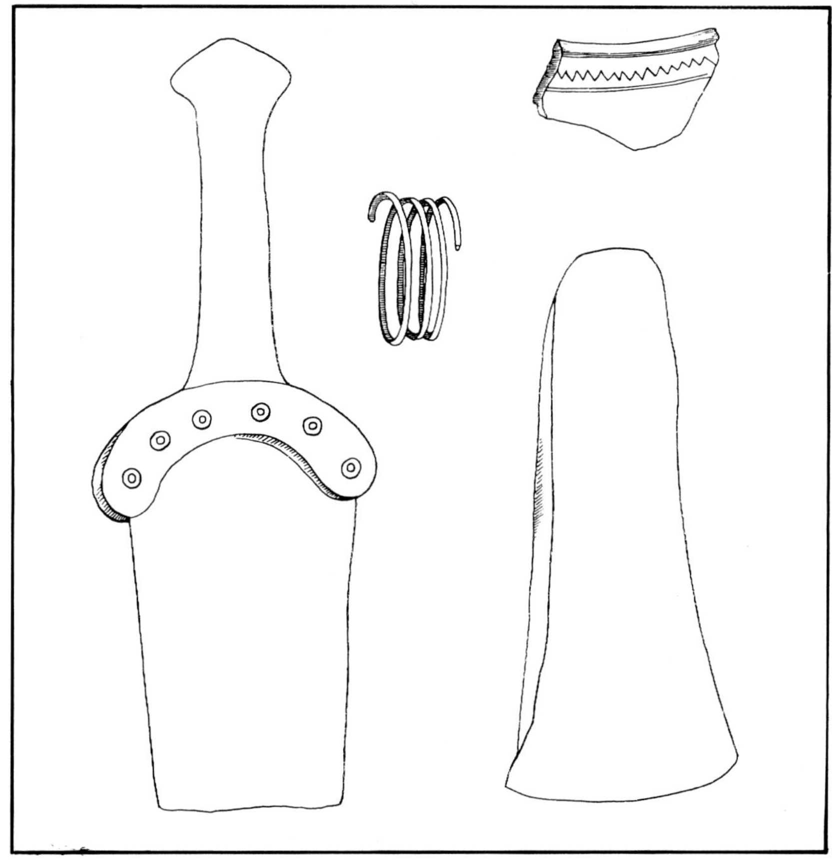

The vanished treasure of Singleyrac tomb. *(Based on a 19th century illustration). A number of grave goods were found in close proximity to a buried skeleton in a stone-walled tomb at Singleyrac; these included a bronze hilted sword, a flat axe, a dozen gold spirals forming a necklace, a gold baguette, and a sherd of pottery. The present location of these objects is unknown.*

Was this yet another princely tomb, albeit a bit later? Human bones and the skeletal remains of a horse were said to have accompanied a beautiful sword from the marshes of the river Lizonne, in the north of the Périgord, and was once attributed to Saint-Paul Lizonne, then to Bouteilles-Saint-Sébastien, then to Allemans, and later even to Saint-Séverin in Charente. The sword has an 84 centimeter-long, acute blade and was riveted to a bronze hilt. The pommel is mushroom shaped, the hilt was trifoliate, and thin incised fanlike grooves decorate the blade itself. This bronzesmith's masterpiece is an exceptional weapon and can only compare to a handful of others distributed throughout France: the Doubs (Reugney), Puy-de-Dôme (Pont-du-Château), Haute-Loire (Cheylounet Saint-Vidal), Tarn-et-Garonne (Castelsarrasin), and Aude (Sigean). The gold spiral from Le Grand Roc in Les Eyzies must also be from the Early or Middle Bronze Age, although it was discovered in a swallow-hole with much later objects. It reveals again how much wealth had accumulated in a few hands. Other tombs were more modest. The skeleton at the grotte des Partisans at Marquay, for example, was simply laid or dropped into a narrow gallery and covered with a pile of stones. The only offerings associated with it are a few potsherds.

Decorated blade of a bronze dagger from Coux-et-Bigaroque (private collection).
The dagger-blade decorated by punch and line patterns was inspired by the Early Bronze Age Rhone culture.

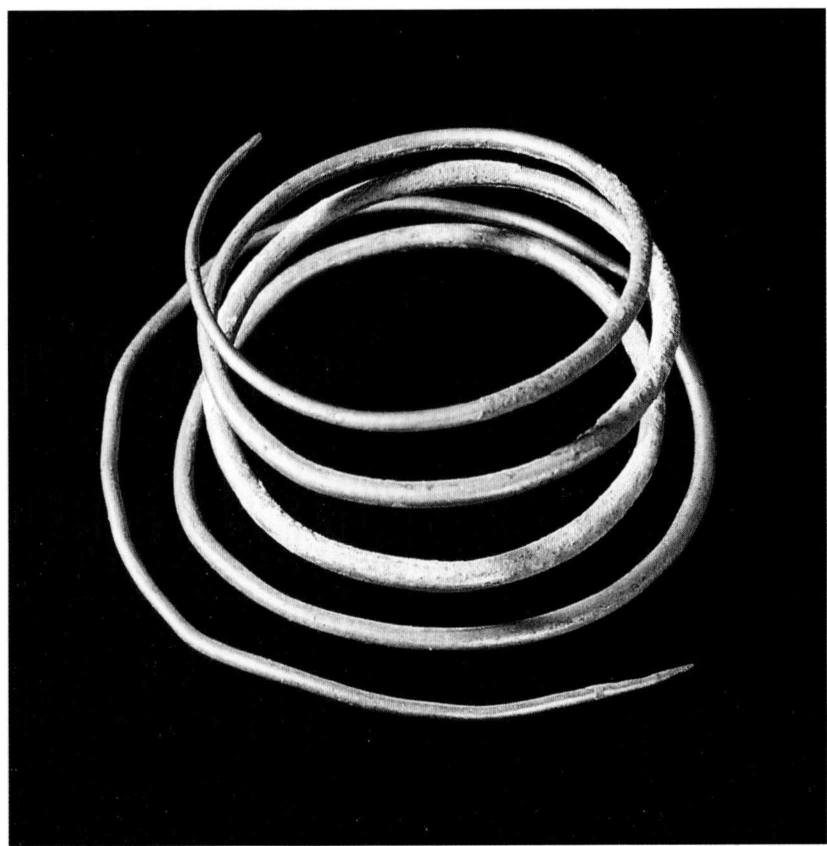

The golden spiral from Laugerie-Basse (Laugerie-Basse Museum). *This spiral made from a long gold wire with pointed ends and shaped into a coil, was discovered in an almost inaccessible hollow of a cliff at Le Grand Roc near Laugerie-Basse.*

Bronze sword from Saint-Paul-de-Lizonne (Musée du Périgord). *This magnificent bronze-hilted sword is 84 centimeters long and was discovered near the marshlands of Lizonne along with the bones of a horse. This very rare type from the Early Middle Bronze Age is also found in the Massif Central region and Languedoc.*

The grotte des Partisans near Marquay. *Several years ago, an Early Bronze Age burial was found and excavated in the grotte des Partisans at Marquay in the Beune valley.*

The Early Bronze Age skeleton from the grotte des Partisans *(excavation by J. Roussot-Larroque and J.M. Mormone). The skeleton laid in a very shallow pit in a descending corridor, and in a very poor state of preservation due to the visitor traffic. It was found in association with charcoal and pottery from the Early Bronze Age. The entire assemblage was dated to 1,600 B.C.*

Prosperity in the Middle Bronze Age: weapons and ornaments

As early as the mid second millennium B.C., bronze objects in increasing number were cast, hammered into shape, and sometimes decorated with engraved patterns. Axes, daggers, swords, or bracelets were very rare in living sites and are found above all in hoards, ritual deposits, private treasures, or in the founders' hoards awaiting recovery or resmelting. These hoards are spread throughout the Périgord region; from the north (La Rochebeaucourt), and Ribéracois (Vanxains), to the Isle basin (Coulaures; Saint-Front-de-Pradoux; Mussidan), from the Upper Vézère (Hautefort), the Vézère proper (Thonac, Fleurac, Meyrals) and from the Dordogne (Berbiguières), to the south of the Périgord (Issigeac).

As in nearby Gironde, flanged axes were the dominant type. Local forms like the Thonac axe emerged with a narrow top, a wider cutting edge, and concave flanges, which were also present at Rouffignac and Vanxains. V-shaped grooves were hammered onto the surface of some of the axes. A sample of unused smelted axes from the same cast suggests that itinerant bronzesmiths worked in the Périgord at the time. As far as palstaves are concerned, different forms existed side by side, some resembling the Atlantic types and others comparable to the interior, Limousin or Massif Central regions. Both types are sometimes found in the hoards (Hautefort, Fleurac). The bracelets from the Middle Bronze Age are solid armlets with slightly thicker ends. They are decorated with incised geometric patterns of ladders, chevrons, and triangles. Some deposits contain only bracelets (La Rochebeaucourt-et-Argentine; La Calévie cave in Meyrals); others may contain axes and bracelets (Fleurac). One example of an isolated bracelet was found in the Gorge d'Enfer in Les Eyzies. Some were worn in a series like our own "semainier" French bracelet in which seven bracelets represent the days of the week. In the case of the

Middle Bronze Age bracelet from the grotte de la Calévie at Meyrals *(discovered by the Spéléo-Club of Périgueux, Musée du Périgord). Four bracelets with incised decorations were found in 1974 in the grotte de la Calévie. Together they form a single unit; each bracelet is slightly wider than the next and is designed to be worn in succession on the forearm. The largest and the smallest were decorated with the same pattern of hatched triangles (our photograph). The two middle sized were decorated differently.*

Detail of the engraved decoration on the bronze bracelet from Calévie. *This bracelet is one of the two central pieces of this composition. Each panel is separated by vertical line pattern, a characteristic of the local Middle Bronze Age.*

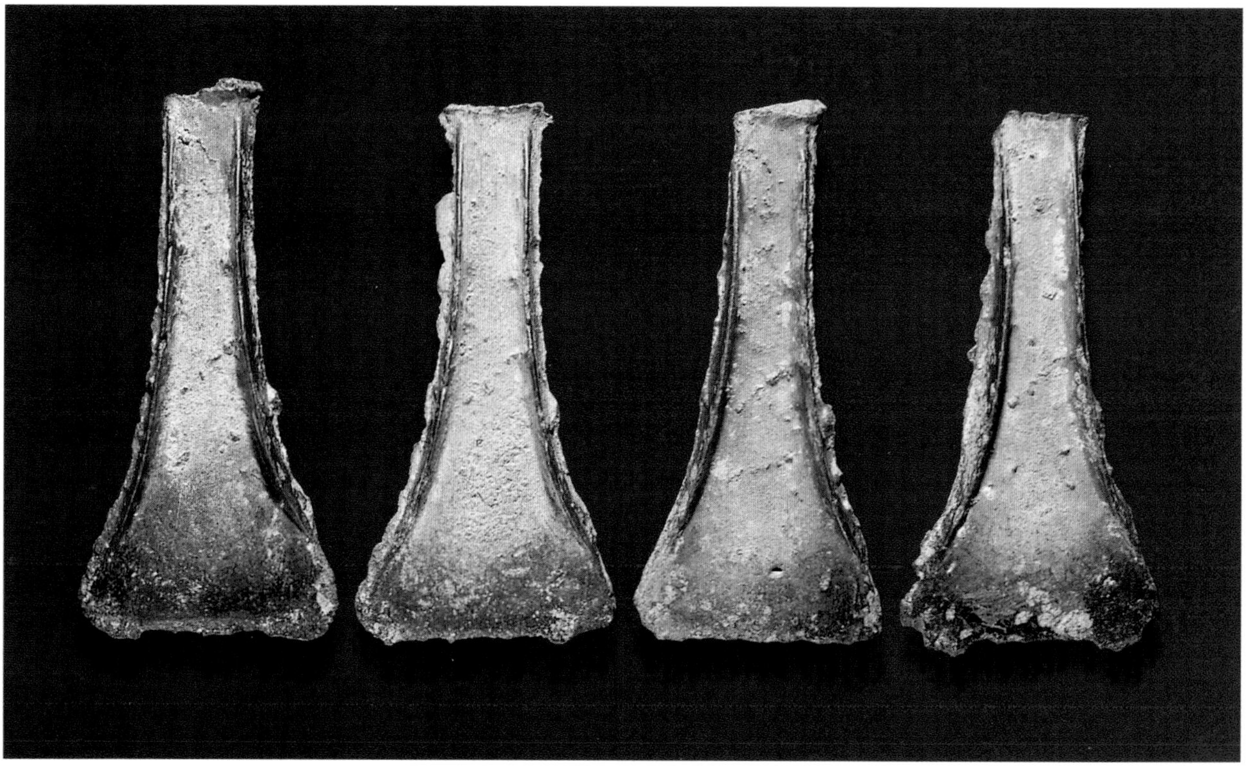

The hoard of bronze axes from Thonac (private collection). *Twenty-seven newly smelted flanged celts from the Middle Bronze age were discovered at Thonac in the 1930s. Due to certain identical defects which were reproduced, it is clear that the specimens featured in the photograph were cast from the same lay-out. Their special shape, (the "Thonac type"), suggests that they were made by Périgord bronze founders.*

The hoard of bronze axes at Vanxains. *Discovered a dozen years ago at Vanxains, flanged axes and palstaves from the Middle Bronze Age had been buried in a pit. Some of the flanged axes resemble those of Thonac.*

La Roque-Saint-Christophe at Peyzac-le-Moustier. *An impressive limestone cliff with its rock-shelters overlooks the left bank of the Vézère River at Le Moustier. The rock-shelters located at river level were occupied in the Upper Périgordian period of the Upper Paleolithic, the Neolithic, the Bronze Age, and through to the Middle Ages. The stratified levels of the Middle and Late Bronze Age are very important for the study of these periods in the Périgord region.*

La Roque-Saint-Christophe. *A deep rock-shelter at the base of the imposing cliff of Roque- Saint-Christophe was occupied throughout prehistory and even up to the French Revolution.*

Meyrals' bracelets, four were worn in order of size; two of them had identical decorations. The heaviest bracelet weighs 427 grams, which goes to show the lengths to which a Bronze Age beauty would go in the name of fashion! The typical decorations of the period were panels separated by vertical lines (Les Eyzies, Meyrals, and Fleurac). This style was then widespread in the French west and southwest including Brittany, Angoumois, Médoc, Agenais, but may have originated in more inland, continental regions.

For reasons unknown, weapons, daggers, swords, and spear points are not found in association with axes or bracelets in these Périgordian deposits. Only the dredging of streams have brought them to light, though dredging has been less intense here than in other regions. With the exception of a few isolated pieces, it is principally at Bergerac, at Le Fleix, and at Port-Sainte-Foy-et-Ponchapt that the dredging of the Dordogne has yielded an interesting series of weapons from the Middle Bronze Age. It is not unusual to find trapeze-butted daggers with two or often four rivets. One was found at Fleix and four at Port-Sainte-Foy, where a two-riveted sword with a wide blade was also found. These weapons are obviously related to those from the Middle Bronze Age Tumulus culture usually found in southwest Germany and Alsace, as well as the Massif Central, and just inside central-western France and the Gironde.

Magnificent socketed spear points have also been recovered from the Dordogne River. These include a 43.5 cm long, Sucy-en-Brie type spear-point from Fleix, and spear points at times decorated by punch and lines from Port-Sainte-Foy. Two among them have basal loops, a British style imitated in France, since a cast for a spear of this type was found at Vilhonneur in Charente. Certain spears from the Dordogne still contained sections of wooden hafts in their sockets. The meeting of characteristics of various cultural traditions in one place demonstrates the importance of the Dordogne valley as a cross-roads of influence in the Bronze Age.

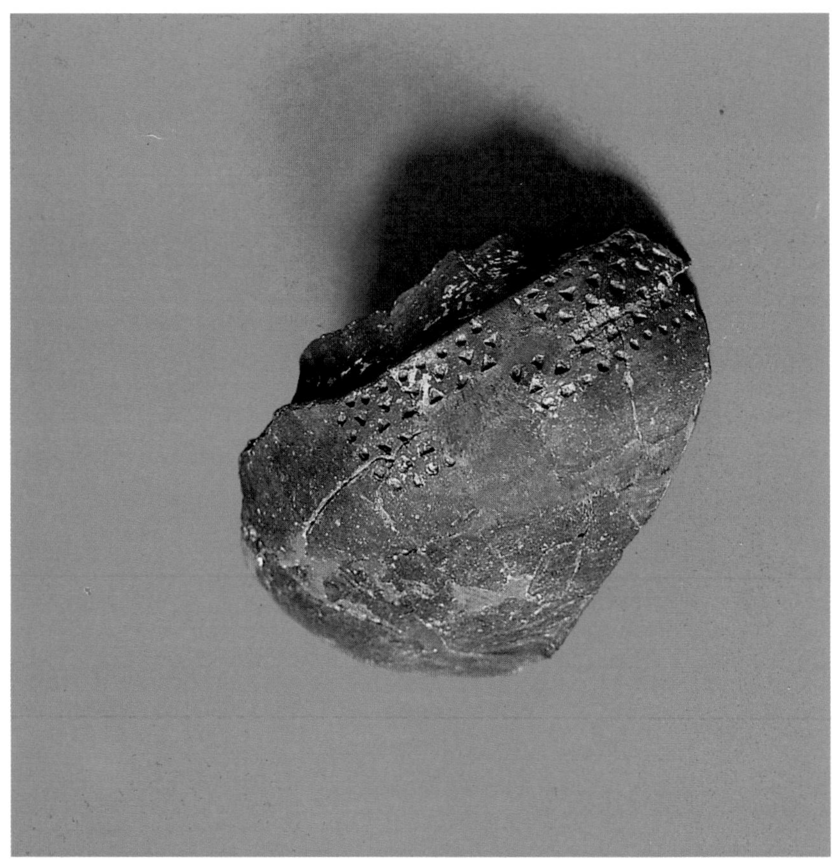

La Roque Saint-Christophe, Middle Bronze Age ceramics *(excavations of J. Roussot-Larroque). The pots decorated with excised or incised patterns from Roque Saint-Christophe, like this large jug fragment, were inspired by the Tumulus culture of eastern France. The stamped motives may have been in-laid in white.*

Settlements of this period remain sporadically known in the Périgord. In the Dordogne valley not far from Port-Sainte-Foy, and in a large part of the central-west and the south-west, Médoc style pottery decorated with applied cordons and rustication were very popular. House sites are practically unknown in this sector except for a few ashy areas. The influence of this pottery style extended inland at least as far as the Les Eyzies region. In the Vézère valley, one of the most picturesque habitation sites is located in one of the lower rock-shelters at the foot of the high cliffs of Roque-Saint-Christophe beside a ford in the Vézère at Peyzac-Le Moustier. Under the natural protection of these deep rock-shelters, Middle Bronze Age people abutted flimsy shelters against boulders and fallen rubble. These structures were supported by beams of wood, the traces of which were uncovered during the first excavations. The report suggest the presence of a small, round house. Unfortunately, subsequent occupations in the final Bronze and Middle Ages, as well as earlier and sometimes destructive excavations of the site, left very few vestiges of this dwelling. The pottery was made on location and included large pot-bellied earthenware jars, jugs either undecorated or with applied cordons, cups and beakers, at times burnished, with incised or punctuated patterns, and vases with small feet. One level, C 14 dated to 3,040 +/- 120 B.P. (or about 1,430

Decorated Middle Bronze Age vase from the grotte Vaufrey *(excavation by Jean-Philippe Rigaud). Grotte Vaufrey is a cave in the Comte cliff face. Bronze Age pottery, in a style similar to that of Quercy, was unearthed in the upper layers: for example, this cup with incised chevrons.*

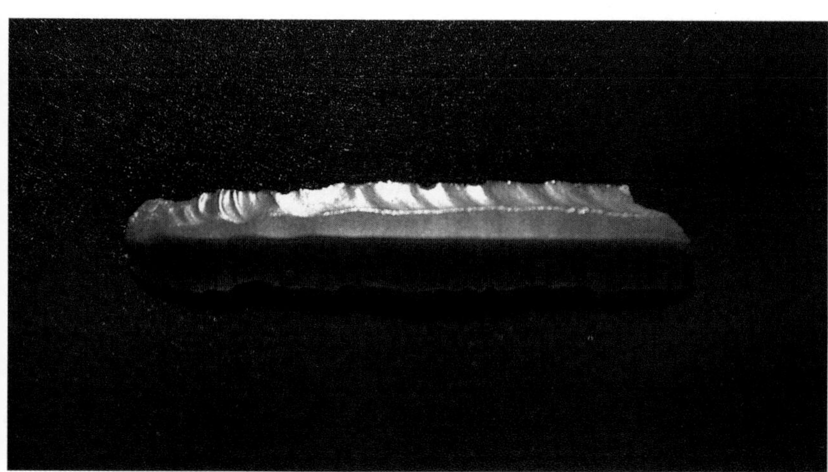

Yellow flint blade with plant polish from grotte Vaufrey (dorsal view) *(excavation by Jean-Philippe Rigaud). This broken blade, made from a translucent yellow flint, bears a shiny luster or "plant polish" on its right side, which indicates that the object was used to cut silicious stems like grain stalks or reeds for example.*

to 1,120 B.C.) yielded vases with incised or excised triangles, diamonds, or squares in-laid in white. This ceramic style reveals some of the same continental influences of the Tumulus culture which were already visible in the production of metal objects such as trapeze hilted swords and daggers dredged from the Dordogne. Beds of ashes containing bronze drops and pieces of slag suggest that metalworking associated with the Middle Bronze Age layers at this living site. A bronze flanged axe - a miniature reproduction of the Thonac celts - was discovered in the Combe de Banne near Roque Saint-Christophe.

The importance of the Vézère Valley in the Middle Bronze Age, especially in the Les Eyzies region, is reinforced by other finds. During work at Font de Gaume, a set of impressive objects were discovered. These included a barbed and tanged bone arrow, a pendant of the type found at Roque Saint-Christophe, a beautiful toggle-pin with a thread-hole and engraved decoration, a handled cup, and a polypod vessel. The pin, which is typical of the Tumulus culture, resembles the work of bronze workshops from the west bank of the Rhine. Why were these objects deposited deep within a cave gallery? Were they associated with a burial? As in other karst regions, the inhabitants of the Middle Bronze Age Périgord regularly visited the underground networks of caves, either to occupy them temporarily (perhaps in times of insecurity) or to carry out mysterious activities linked to some Chtonic cult. Rouffignac cave is one example of this. Although Bronze Age people may have been impressed by the Paleolithic paintings, they also sometimes decorated the caves themselves.

In the southern Périgord, caves and rock-shelters were also regularly visited. This area, along with the nearby Quercy, forms a small province with its own characteristic ceramic style. Here bronze is apparently even more scarce in the settlements, while pottery is more common including polypod vessels, cups and urns, with rich decorations incised or

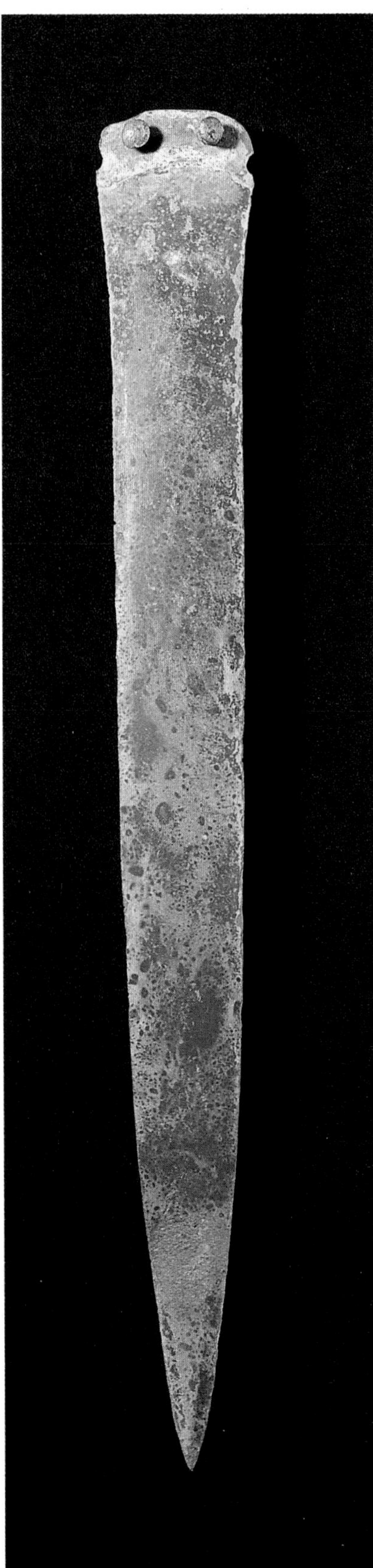

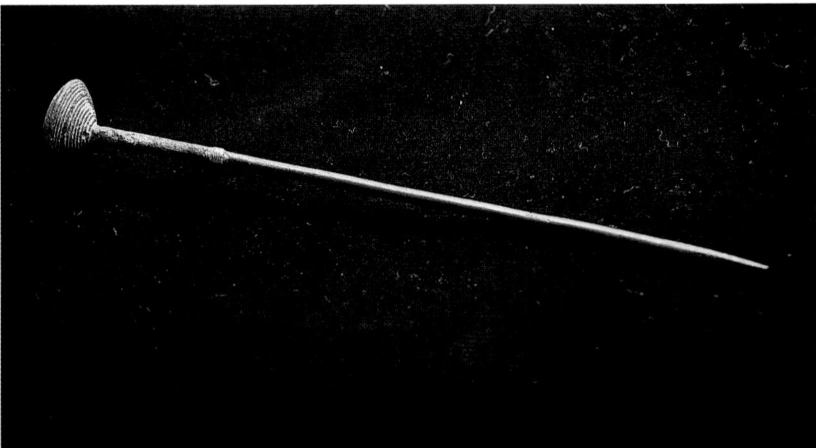

Bronze disc-headed pin from Toulon in Périgueux (Musée du Périgord). *Found with a decorated spear point, this pin has a decorated discoidal head smithed separately from the shaft. These Final Bronze Age pins are usually found in the eastern half of France, from the upper valley of the Seine and the Yonne, to the Middle Rhône.*

punctuated, but rarely stamped. In the cliff-dwellings of Le Comte, at the confluence of the Céou and the Dordogne Rivers, vases of this type were found with herring bone or hatched triangle motifs. Human bones and even a child's burial were found. There do not seem to have been any borders between the southeastern Périgord and the Vézère Valley, which adopted and possibly even produced southern style pottery like the polypod vases of Font-de-Gaume and Roque-Saint-Christophe.

A few hill settlements were found in the Sarlat area at Roc de Saint-Augustin near Carsac de Carlux. Reave systems may have their origin from dry-stone ancient structures of that time. Without systematic research of the area, it is impossible to distinguish prehistoric, medieval or more recent dry-stone walls from the Bronze age constructions. The excavation of Roque-Saint-Christophe revealed that animal husbandry was practiced and that pork was the meat of choice in Périgord cuisine. The hunting of red deer, roe deer, and boar, in addition to fishing, added variety to the standard diet.

A preview of the Final Bronze Age

Near the end of the second millennium, without changing their place of residence, the inhabitants of Roque Saint-Christophe adopted new techniques once again originating from farther inland. This is best reflected in the ceramics which are sensitive barometers to any change. In the early stages of the Final Bronze Age, cups and carinated bowls with offset rims emerged, decorated with horizontal or vertical rilling and sometimes with warts or buckles surrounded by rills as in Yonne or in the Western-Alpine regions. This style appears to replace stamped or excised ware.

The same inspiration is observed in metal objects such as the median-winged axe of Villars, the disc-headed pin from Toulon in Périgueux, (found with an impressively

Middle Bronze Age sword from the Dordogne river at Port-Sainte-Foy (private collection). *Dredged from the Dordogne, this two-riveted sword bears the traces of a missing hilt which was probably made of wood.*

Decorated bronze spear-point from Toulon near Périgueux (Musée du Périgord). *Discovered in 1889 along with a bronze pin at l'Hermitage du Toulon near Périgueux, this spear-point is decorated quite elaborately with incised, lines, dots and herring bone patterns on the wings and base of the socket.*

Roque-Saint-Christophe: excavation of a Final Bronze Age level *(excavation by Julia Roussot-Larroque). In one of the lower rock-shelters of Roque-Saint-Christophe, surface of a Final Bronze Age level. Here we see the fragments of a dish painted in red and a meander-decorated vase.*

decorated spear point), and the Rixheim type sword dredged from the Dordogne River at Port-Sainte-Foy. A superb bronze-hilted sword, also dredged from the Dordogne River at Port-Saint-Foy, is a rare type which dates to slightly later period.

The heyday of the Périgord Bronze Age

At the turn of the first millennium B.C., the great trends which marked the start of the Final Bronze Age reached the Périgord region, which, for the next three centuries, was strongly influenced by what came to be known as the "Urnfields culture". Ceramics achieved a higher quality. Fine wares consisted of refined pastes, thin walls, and vessels with a shiny black or sometimes light beige slip. The shapes were influenced by bronze sheet vessels and included simple, segmented, or carinated profiles, oblique rims, cylindrical necks, etc. Some cups are omphalos-based and fluted or combed decorations take on subtle mastery of the art of pottery making. It seems that they were soon adopted in a large part of France from the east to the central-west and the south. Ceramicists in the Périgord skillfully reproduced this art form and their works rivaled those of the interior, the Upper Rhine, Switzerland, and eastern France. A few prototypes may have been transported over the Massif Central, but the bulk of production was centered in the Périgord proper. At Roque Saint-Christophe, some of the caves, perched high in the cliff wall, contained natural clay deposits with calcite inclusions. Pestles were found in some of the occupation layers. These had been used to reduce burned quartz cobbles into a fine powder which was then used as grit. Pottery kilns must have been located someplace nearby. A few of the most impressive vases, like the one at Reignac near Tursac, had inlaid bands of tin. They even made clay bracelets which were occasionally decorated in the same fashion as the lignite rings.

***Cave dwellings near Les Eyzies.** Almost at the top of cliffs, natural caves, sometimes recut, has been used during war-time. Bronze Age remains has been also discovered there.*

The riverside populations of the Vézère and the Dordogne continued to seek out caves sites. Larger sites like Roque-Saint-Christophe were still well within the light of day, and many rock-shelters were re-occupied at this time (e.g. Reignac, Laugerie-Basse). As before, deep caverns (Rouffignac and grotte de la Martine near Domme), inhospitable underground streams (Fontanguillère), or caves with nearly inaccessible galleries (grotte de l'Eglise de Guilhem at Les Eyzies) were frequented for other reasons. The presence of querns and large cordoned urns used for storage indicates that agriculture was in full swing. There is also evidence that cattle, pigs, as well as sheep or goats were raised. The people of the Final Bronze Age also took delight in the hunt. At Roque-Saint-Christophe, one of the trophies, a curved boar tusk, was at least 18 cm. long, and a perforated bone arrowpoint is believed to have been used to hunt birds.

Few tombs date to this period. Two skeletons were laid head to foot, in the northern most part of the Grand Abri at Roque-Saint-Christophe. A sizeable number of human skeletal remains - some say as many as 200 skulls! - were recovered from an underground stream at Fontanguillère. The bodies are believed to have been laid on wooden platforms. Unfortunately, these remains were damaged by successive floods and by decades of uncontrolled excavations, and it is impossible to determine the true age of these structures or their significance. Perhaps, as in the case of grotte de Han in Belgium, it involved a water cult sanctuary. In the deep recesses of Rouffignac, pottery deposits are sometimes accompanied by a handful of ashes. Could this have involved some sort of cremation? Grotte de la Maurélie in Plazac, immediately adjacent to Rouffignac, contained whole clay pots associated with a pin, and a bronze bracelet. These vases do not seem to have contained cremations, and only one or two human bones were found in the vicinity. It is unlikely that people used caves as living sites, even on a temporary basis. Instead, we imagine that these areas were used for mysterious rituals or possibly funerary rites as in the grotte de Rancogne in Charente.

Metal is often rare in these sites with the exception of small objects like knifes, arrowpoints, and the pins of Roque-Saint-Christophe and Laugerie-Basse. Most of the weapons, tools, and ornaments were recovered and resmelted to respond to new styles of the times. Our concept is drawn from only a few isolated grave goods and dredged objects, since very few metal goods from this period were deposited in this area. The site of Saint-Front-de-Pradoux contained only two end winged axes with a loop and the fragments of four other axes including palstaves and socketed celts of a type which was also found in Gironde. Other isolated objects include continental types like the winged axe of Les Eyzies, which resemble Swiss models associated with "Rhine-Swiss-Eastern France" pottery from surrounding areas. The same influences are visible in ornaments such as pins, belt or chest plates, pendants, and small bracelets at Fontanguillère.

Influences from the west, however, are seen in three pistilliform Atlantic swords, one from the Isle Valley at Périgueux, the second from the Dordogne Valley near Saint-Cyprien, and the third from Fontanguillère. The region was a pivotal center for bronzesmiths of the Atlantic and the interior where comparable swords found in Limousin (Louignac in Corrèze) and in Auvergne (Limoise in Allier) trace a route back to the Saône valley and Switzerland.

The end of the Bronze Age in the Périgord.

The latest phase of the Bronze Age (from 900 to 800 B.C.) was a continuation of the period that preceded it. The same living sites were continuously occupied and even some hill sites were re-occupied. The ceramics were still of the same high quality that characterized the previous phase. The "fine wares" often with a black burnished slip still bore the horizontal lines made by a two or three-pronged comb. In general, ceramic forms became simplified and rounded. A typical vase of this period is the "onion bulb" gobelet, with oblique rims, a rounded belly, and a narrow base, which became widespread in the Périgord, in the valley of the Dordogne (Castelréal in Urval), Vézère (Roque Saint-Christophe, Laugerie-Basse), and the Isle (Puypinsou). The meanders or Greek key-patterns which appeared earlier, adorned cups and rimless bowls. The vessels" interiors were decorated with concentric fluting or printed panels alternating with smooth areas. A carmine red made from haematite was used to decorate some vases. The most beautiful vessels were decorated with black and red concentric circles.

Metal objects are a rarity in living sites. However, judging from the slag and ashes found at Laugerie-Basse and elsewhere, artisans must have smelted some bronze there. There are very few deposits from this period in the Périgord. A few isolated finds including a carp's tongue sword from Saint-Léon-sur-l'Isle, Armorican socketed axes from Roque-Saint-Christophe and Ecorneboeuf near Périgueux, and the small earrings in gold plated bronze from Fontanguillère are evidence of contact with regions on the Atlantic. A large bronze flesh skewer dredged from the Dordogne River, evokes images of great banquets at which roasted meat was served.

Tombs are just as rare as they were in the preceding phase. Beneath the entrance to Rouffignac cave, a burned area which had been repeatedly

Protohistoric rock-carvings at Gaussen. *Are the cross-bow like rock-carvings in Gaussen cave proto historic? Without any context, it is impossible to be certain, but the bow and "phi" signs are also found in the cave art of the Neolithic and Bronze Age.*

Fords in the Vézère River on the road from Le Bugue to Les Eyzies-de-Tayac *(following pages). Fords, an obligatory means of passage before the modern road system, are often sources of archaeological artifacts, particularly bronze objects, lost or thrown in as an offering by those crossing the waterways.*

An electrum earring from the Tuckey tumulus at Lanouaille (private collection). *A large, stone-based, earthen barrow contained an Early Iron Age cremation with graphite-painted vases, the remains of a sheet bronze vessel with suspended rings, and an earring made from electrum (an alloy of gold and silver). The filigree technology with soldered beads of gold originated in the Mediterranean basin.*

dug out and paved with stones, and which contained human bones, is believed to be a pyre. In the same area, a final Bronze Age bronze button was found. In a deep gallery of the same cave, a (ritual?) deposit containing a bronze spear point and other buttons (resembling the brass buttons of a uniform), were also discovered. Similar objects associated with rings were found in a hoard at La Croix at Terrasson.

Towards new beginnings: The First Iron Age in the Périgord

From the end of 8th century B.C., iron gradually began to compete with bronze. A good example of this technological transition is a sword with an iron blade and a bronze grip dredged from the Dordogne at Port-Saint-Foy. Bronze and iron swords were used briefly in equal measure before iron definitively became the metal of choice. This innovation proved quite beneficial to the Périgord which was a rich source of iron ore (mined until the turn of the 20th century). It offered easy access to surface deposits of oxidized ore which were then easily smelted by the still rudimentary methods of the Early Iron Age. This new technology, diffused by the Hittites in the Eastern Mediterranean, soon spread througout Central Europe and the Balkans. Its western diffusion had long been attributed to mounted Thraco-Cimmerians. These horsemen, recognized for their swords and distinctive horse gear were believed to have introduced (or reintroduced) the practice of barrow burials. The trail of Early Iron Age mounds indicates the path of their incursions around the southern slopes of the Massif Central, across the Plateaux of Cantal, through Lozère, Quercy, and on

Pedestalled urn with graphite decoration from Jumilhac-le-Grand (Musée du Périgord). *An urn filled with cremated human bones from a mound at Lande de Prunou near Jumilhac-le-Grand. The graphite geometric design is characteristic of the Early Iron Age in the Eastern Périgord, Limousin, and Charente.*

to Limousin and the Périgord. Whether such a long Trans-European migration ever took place is now somewhat controversial. Some regional peculiarities distinguish these populations of the Early Iron Age which were deeply rooted in the terminal phase of the Final Bronze Age.

However around the 7th or 6th century B.C., settlements, which had been continuously occupied since the Bronze Age, were abandoned. From then on, people preferred to occupy hilltop sites like Ecorneboeuf. These settlement locations provided a strategic and defensive advantage which might explain why they were sought out. Another possible explanation is that climatic conditions around 800 B.C. made some dwelling places uninhabitable in the humid valleys. Systems of walls were erected, and ditches were sometimes cut into the rock to protect dwellings, perched high on the hills of the Périgord and surrounding regions.

The dead were buried under tumuli or barrows sometimes consisting of a pile of stones which protected a central chamber (Landes de Prunou in Jumilhac-le-Grand), with a circle of stones placed around the mound as in the Limousin - a style which is also found in eastern Périgord. The deceased were burned on funerary pyres, and the cremated bones were collected, perhaps washed, and then placed in ceramic urns along with metal objects, weapons, or ornaments. The mound was sometimes placed directly on top of the pyre. The vessels were fine and quite elegant with high necks (Jumilhac-le-Grand), and sometimes supported by a pedestal. Decorations were painted in graphite (the source material was found in the Limousin). Complex, silver-grey, geometric patterns were brought out against a brown background. The inspiration for this technique must have come from Central Europe, Southern Austria, and Slovakia where Early Iron Age urns were graphite-painted. These "fine wares" were not restricted to use in funerary ritual, as they are also sometimes found in settlements (Ecorneboeuf). Some of the deceased obviously had high social status, like the person to whom the great mound of Tuckey was dedicated at Lanouaille. This impressive tumulus, (over 25 meters diameter and almost 4 meters high), contained four graphite-painted vases, the very decomposed remains of a sheet-bronze vessel with suspended rings, and a magnificent earring made of electrum - an alloy of gold and silver. The design for this unique filigree earring, decorated with gold beads, was inspired by Mediterranean goldsmiths - possibly Etruscans. The bronze vase may also come from the Mediterranean. Thus, as early as the sixth century B.C., there existed a wealthy aristocracy, in more or less direct contact with the cultural centers of Central Europe and Northern Italy.

THE REAL FACE OF THE PERIGORD

Over the millennia of prehistory and protohistory, the face of the Périgord have been modelled, little by little, under the influence of the people who lived here. From flaked pebbles to cave art, from stone to bronze, and then to iron, the entire region gradually developed its own unique personality. After the magnificent accomplishment of the prehistoric "Sistine Chapels", the Périgord did not fall back into obscurity, as one might have thought. Its place in more recent prehistory and proto-history, all too often ignored, foreshadowed the important role this region later played in pre-Roman Gaul.

La Gonterie-Boulouneix, Le Roc Plat. *A hill site blocked off by a rampart, Le Roc Plat was perhaps an oppidum (or fortified residence) during the Iron Age.*

***Houses at Breuilh near Marquay.** These picturesque stone houses are not Gaullois, as they were built only a few hundred years ago. Nevertheless, they may reflect what some protohistoric Périgord houses looked like. None of the houses dating to this period exists today.*

Archaeological park in Beynac and a reconstitution of a Gaul house.

Caves, rock-shelters, and sites: open to the public.

Sites with an asterix are normally open year round (for guided tours).

Bara-Bahau*, Le Bugue. Cave with wall engravings.
Bernifal, Meyrals. Cave with wall engravings and paintings.
Beynac. Archaeological park and museum, from the Neolithic to the Gauls. Reconstituted living structures and monuments.
Cap Blanc, Marquay. Rock-shelter with wall sculptures; reconstituted Magdalenian burial.
Castelmerle, Sergeac. Visit: Labattut, Reverdit, la Souquette. Site museum at the Castelmerle auberge.
Les Combarelles*, Les Eyzies-de-Tayac. Cave with wall engravings.
Cro Magnon, Les Eyzies-de-Tayac. Rock-shelter visible from the road near the hotel of the same name.
La Ferrassie, Savignac-de-Miremont. Rock-shelter, control sections. Site is visible from the road.
Font de Gaume*, Les Eyzies-de-Tayac. Cave with wall engravings and paintings.
Fourneau du Diable, Bourdeilles. Fenced off prehistoric site. Visible from the roadside.
Gorge d'Enfer, les Eyzies-de-Tayac. Guided tour of a prehistoric site (see also : Abri du Poisson and Abri Lartet).
La Grèze, Marquay. Cave with wall engravings. Site visited via the Musée national de Préhistoire.
Abri Labattut, Sergeac. Rock-shelter at Castelmerle.
Abri Lartet, Les Eyzies-de-Tayac. Rock-shelter at Gorge d'Enfer.
Lascaux II*, Montignac. Facsimile of the first two galleries of the cave. Museum presentation in the entrance hall.
Laugerie-Basse, Les Eyzies-de-Tayac. Two rock-shelters: Laugerie-Basse and Abri des Marseilles.

Laugerie-Haute, Les Eyzies-de-Tayac. Rock-shelter, control sections.
La Madeleine, Tursac. Enclosed rock-shelter, visible from the outside.
La Micoque, Les Eyzies. Enclosed rock-shelter, visible from the outside.
Le Moustier, Peyzac-le-Moustier. Enclosed rock-shelter, visible from the outside. Located in the village.
Abri Pataud*, Les Eyzies-de-Tayac. Prehistoric site beneath the Pataud rock-shelter. Site museum and wall engraving under the second rock-shelter or Pataud cellar. Human skeletons from the Périgordian VII. Below, the Vignaud site is visible from the road.
Abri du Poisson, Les Eyzies-de-Tayac. Rock-shelter with wall engravings at Gorge d'enfer. Site is visited via Laugerie-Haute.
Préhisto-park, Tursac. In a pleasant atmosphere, several "scenes of prehistoric life" have been reconstituted under the supervision of Professeur Heim.
Régourdou, Montignac. Prehistoric site in which a Neandertal burial was discovered. Small site museum and living bears.
Abri Reverdit, Sergeac. Rock-shelter with wall sculptures at Castelmerle. Partial control section of the site's stratigraphy.
Roque-Saint-Christophe, Peyzac-le-Moustier. Prehistoric rock-shelter at the base of a cliff (which is visible from the road), and historic cliff dwellings. Small prehistoric and historic collection.
Rouffignac, Cave with wall engravings and paintings. Visit by electric train.
Le Ruth, Tursac (on a small back road from Le Moustier). Prehistoric site and small prehistoric collection.
Saint-Cirq-du-Bugue*. Cave with wall engravings and sculptures. Small site museum.
La Souquette, Sergeac. Rock-shelter at Castelmerle.
Le Thot*, Thonac. Prehistoric art exhibit, animal park, and reconstitution of prehistoric campsites and scenes from daily prehistoric life.
Vignaud, Les Eyzies-de-Tayac. Visible from the road.
Teyjat (Grotte de la Mairie), Teyjat. Cave with wall engravings.
Villars. Cave with wall engravings and paintings.

A scene from the Préhisto-park in Tursac.

Museums

Bergerac. Regional prehistoric collection.
Les Eyzies de Tayac. Musée national de Préhistoire. Reference prehistoric collection. Portable art objects on Aurignacian, Solutrean, and Magdalenian blocks. Human burial from Saint-Germain-la-Rivière (Gironde).
Périgueux. Musée du Périgord. Large pre- and proto-historic collection. Portable art (notably from Raymonden), and Aurignacian paintings and engravings on stone blocks. Human skeletons from Régourdou (Mousterian) and Raymonden (Magdalenian).
Brantôme. Musée Desmoulin. Prehistoric collection of industries and art objects from Rochereil.

Some prehistoric collections from the Périgord are found in a number of museums in France and abroad. Four of them deserve a special note here.
Bordeaux. Musée d'Aquitaine. Bas-reliefs to human representations from Laussel. Sculpted bison from Cap Blanc. Large series of collections from Périgord sites.
Paris. Musée de l'Homme. Human remains from la Ferrassie and Cro Magnon. Large number of prehistoric collections. Portable art, notably from Laugerie-Basse, including the "Impudent-Venus".
Saint-Germain-en-Laye. Musée des Antiquités nationales. Collections from principal Périgord sites. Holds a large percentage of the art objects found in the region (Laugerie-Basse, La Madeleine, Limeuil, Grotte Richard, Teyjat; the Venuses of Sireuil, Tursac and Monpazier).
London. British Museum. Christy collection: a part of the excavations by Lartet and Christy in 1863-64. Industries and works of art from Les Eyzies, Gorge d'Enfer, Laugerie-Basse, and La Madeleine. From the Reverdit collection: decorated bone disk of la Tuilière at Saint-Léon-sur-Vézère.

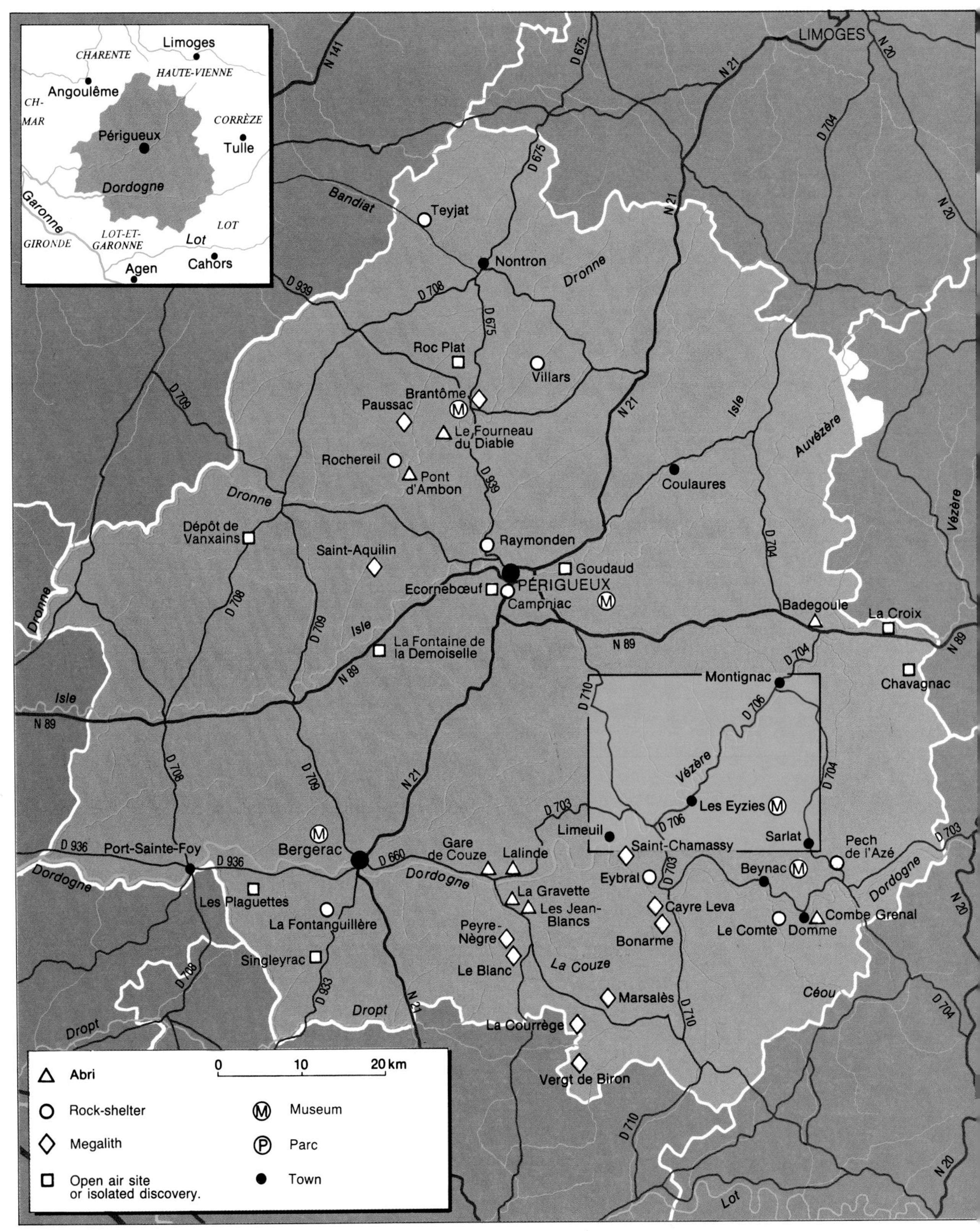

Limoges
CHARENTE
HAUTE-VIENNE
Angoulême
CH-MAR
CORRÈZE
Périgueux
Tulle
Dordogne
Garonne
LOT
GIRONDE
LOT-ET-GARONNE
Lot
Agen
Cahors
LIMOGES
N 141
D 675
N 21
N 20
D 704
Bandiat
Teyjat
Nontron
Dronne
D 939
D 708
Roc Plat
Villars
Brantôme
Paussac
Le Fourneau du Diable
Rochereil
Pont d'Ambon
D 709
Isle
Auvézère
Coulaures
Dépôt de Vanxains
Raymonden
Saint-Aquilin
Goudaud
Ecorneboeuf
PÉRIGUEUX
Campniac
Vézère
Badegoule
La Croix
La Fontaine de la Demoiselle
N 89
Montignac
Chavagnac
D 710
D 706
Les Eyzies
D 703
Limeuil
Sarlat
Pech de l'Azé
Saint-Chamassy
D 936
Port-Sainte-Foy
Bergerac
D 660
Gare de Couze
Lalinde
Eybral
Beynac
Dordogne
La Gravette
Les Jean-Blancs
Cayre Leva
Combe Grenal
Les Plaguettes
La Fontanguillère
Peyre-Nègre
Bonarme
Le Comte
Domme
Singleyrac
Le Blanc
La Couze
Céou
Marsalès
D 933
Dropt
La Courrège
Vergt de Biron
Abri
Rock-shelter
Megalith
Open air site or isolated discovery.
Museum
Parc
Town
0
10
20 km

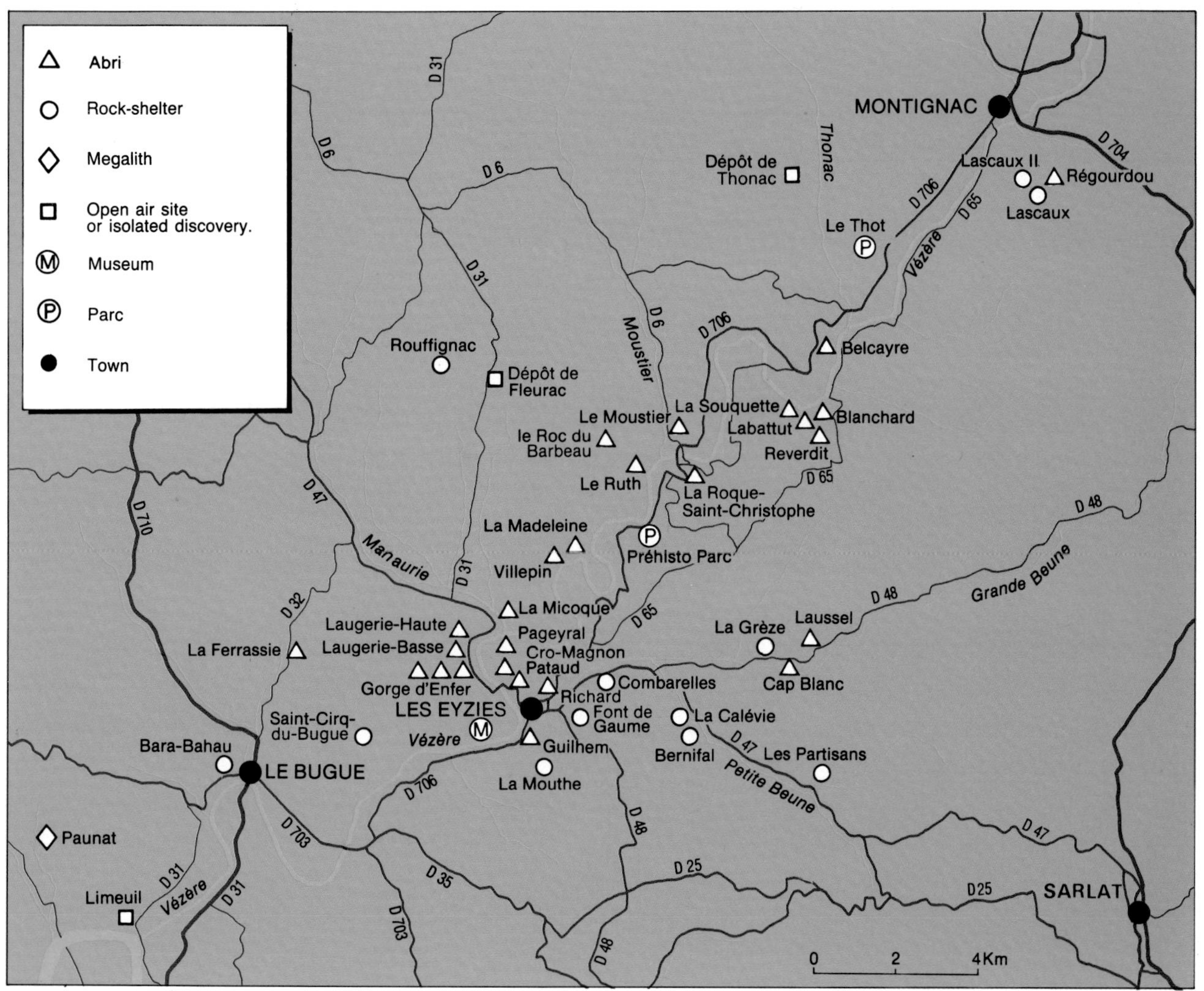

The Périgord, the land of recent prehistory. *A few years ago, the Périgord, now in the Department of Dordogne, was dubbed the "Land of humankind". Of course, it is was not the native land of prehistoric humans, nor the cradle. "Homo habilis" emerged in Africa 2.5 million years ago. However, the Périgord is a country of late prehistoric ' peoples - "Homo sapiens" (Neandertal and Cro-Magnon). Most of the important sites are located along the valleys or at the base of cliffs. This doesn't mean prehistoric humans did not live, as we do, in open air sites, under simple huts covered with animal hides. But they prefered, at least in this region, the rock-shelters which provide a ready made roof and were located nearby abundant game. The first prehistorians, after Lartet and Christy in 1863-64, were mostly interested in these rock-shelters since they Humankind'' are important prehistoric sites which are all too often overshadowed by the Périgord's reputation. These include the small decorated cave of Pair-non-Pair, (with its Gravettian engravings), on the floor of the Dordogne Valley, north of Libourne; the Solutrean site of Roc-de-Sers, located near Angoulême which produced exceptional bas-reliefs (now preserved at Musée des Antiquités nationales at Saint-Germain-en-Laye); and the cave-sanctuaries of Cougnac and Pech-Merle in Quercy, east of Sarlat. A large number of decorated Périgord objects in stone or bone are preserved at distant museums (especially at the Musée des Antiquités nationales in Saint-Germain-en-Laye and the Musée d'Aquitaine in Bordeaux) to which a visit would make the Dordogne experience complete.*

BIBLIOGRAPHY

Periodicals
Archéologia
Bulltins de la Société historique et archéologique du Périgord.
Paléo, revue d'archéologie préhistorique, Les Eyzies.
Les dossiers d'Archéologie.

Books
COLLECTED WORK. *Art et civilisations des chasseurs de la Préhistoire,* 34 000-8 000 av. J.-C. Paris, Laboratoire de Préhistoire du Musée de l'Homme — Muséum d'Histoire naturelle, 1984.
COLLECTED WORK. *L'art des cavernes. Atlas des grottes ornées paléolithiques françaises.* Paris, Ministère de la Culture — Imprimerie Nationale, 1984.
COLLECTED WORK. *Le temps de la Préhistoire.* Société préhistorique française — Edition Archéologia, 1989.
AUJOULAT (N.), GENESTE (J.-M.), RIGAUD (J.-Ph.) et ROUSSOT (A.) — *La Vézère des origines. Sites préhistoriques, grottes ornées et musées.* Paris, Imprimerie nationale éditions, 1991.
BATAILLE (G.). *La peinture préhistorique. Lascaux ou la naissance de l'art.* Genève, Skira, 1986.
BORDES (F.). *Typologie du Paléolithique ancien et moyen.* Paris, Presses du C.N.R.S, 1988.
BREZILLON (M.). *Dictionnaire de la Préhistoire.* Paris, Librairie Larousse, 1969.
DELLUC (B. et G.). *Connaître Lascaux.* Photographies de Ray Delvert. Bordeaux Editions Sud-Ouest, 1989.
DEMOULE (J.-P.). *La France de la Préhistoire. Mille millénaires, des premiers hommes à la conquête romaine.* Paris, Nathan, 1990.
GUILAINE (J.) dir. et alii. *La Préhistoire d'un continent à l'autre.* Paris, Larousse, 1986.
JELINEK (J.). *Encyclopédie illustrée de l'Homme préhistorique.* Paris, Gründ, 1975.
LEROI-GOURHAN (A.). *Les religions de la Préhistoire. Paléolithique.* paris, Presses universitaires de France, 1990.
LEROI-GOURHAN (A.). *Préhistoire de l'art occidental.* Paris, Edition d'art Lucien Mazenod, 1971.
LEROI-GOURHAN (A.) dir. *Dictionnaire de la Préhistoire.* Paris, Presses universitaires de France, 1988.
MILLOTTE (J.-P.) et THEVENIN (A.). *Les racines des Européens, des origines aux Celtes.* Le Coteau, Horvath, 1988.
MORMONE (J.-M.) et HENRIETTE (B.). — *La Vallée de Cro-Magnon au début du siècle.* Toulouse, Loubatières, 1987.
PLASSARD (M.-O. et J.). *La grotte de Rouffignac.* — Bordeaux, Sud-Ouest, 1989.
ROUSSOT (A.), LENOIR (M.) et ROUSSOT-LARROQUE (J.). *Du biface à l'épée. 700 000 ans de Préhistoire en Aquitaine.* Bordeaux, Musée d'Aquitaine, 1991.
SAINT-BLANQUAT (H. de). *Les premiers Français.* Paris, Castermann, 1987.
VIALOU (D.). *Guide des grottes ornées paléolithiques ouvertes au public.* Paris, Masson, 1976.

PHOTO CREDITS

A. ROUSSOT : pp. 3, 13, 16, 18, 19, 20, 21 above, 29, 30, 31, 33 above, 35, 37, 38 below, 50-51, 52, 53 below, 54 below, 56, 65, 67, 71 below, 73, 74-75, 77, 81, 82, 84 below, 88, 89 below, 92, 93, 94, 97, 102, 103, 104, 105, 106, 107, 108 above, 109, 112 left, 114, 116-117, 118, 122, 123, 128. G. DELLUC : pp. 4, 5, 8 above, 11, 13, 15 above, 21 below, 22 below, 23, 24, 25, 26 above, 32, 33 below, 34, 36-37, 39, 42, 45 above, 45 below, 46, 48, 53 above, 54 above, 57, 59 above, 60, 66, 68, 69, 70, 76, 79, 80, 84 above, 87 below, 89 above, 90, 115, 120-121, backcover. J. ROUSSOT-LARROQUE : pp. 91, 95,, 98 below, 99, 100-101, 111, 113 right. B. CABROL : pp. 8 below, 12, 15 below, 22 above, 26 below, 38 above, 87 above, 110. J. PLASSARD : pp. 61, 62-63, 64, 85 below. R. DELVERT : front cover, 40, 43, 44. A. GLORY : pp. 28, 45 middle, 47, 72 (Delluc collection). LALANNE collection : pp. 10, 49. A. LEROI-GOURHAN : pp. 55, 78. G.-M. RENIE : pp. 112 right, 113 left. J. VERTUT : pp. 59 middle, 59 below. P. BARDOU : p. 71 above. CHAUVIN : p. 98 above. CHEVILLOT : p. 108 below. LAVILLE collection : p. 119. D'ERRICO : p. 85 above. Musée des Eyzies : p. 83. RIVIERE collection : p. 9. D. VIALOU : p. 58.

SUMMARY

TWO OR THREE MILLION YEARS :
A BRIEF SUMMARY (B. & G. D.) p. 3

The down of time ..... p. 3
Four succesive human types ..... p. 3
Warm and cold spells ..... p. 5
Place to live ..... p. 6
The great range of animals ..... p. 7

DATES AND PEOPLE(A. R.) ..... p. 8

1. THE LOWER AND MIDDLE PALEOLITHIC. FROM 450,000 TO 35,000 YEARS AGO(A. R.) ..... p. 11

La Micoque ..... p. 14
Le Pech de l'Aze ..... p. 14
Le Moustier ..... p. 14
La Ferrassie ..... p. 16
Regourdou ..... p. 18

2. THE AURIGACIAN AND THE GRAVETTIAN (OR THE UPPER PERIGORDIAN). FROM 35,000 TO 20,000 YEARS AGO (B. & G. D) ..... p. 20

The last Mousterians ..... p. 20
The first Cro-Magnons ..... p. 21
And then came the Gravettians ..... p. 25
Laussel (A. R.) ..... p. 28
Gorge d'Enfer (A. R.) ..... p. 30

3. THE SOLUTREAN AND THE EARLY MAGDALENIAN FROM 21,000 TO 16,000 YEARS AGO (B. et G. D.) ..... p. 37

The days of the Solutreans 18,000-21,000 ..... p. 37
Laugerie-Haute (A. R.) ..... p. 37
Artisans and talented artists ..... p. 41
A comfortable place to live ..... p. 41
The Badegoulians and the first Magdalenians ..... p. 41
A separate culture between the Solutrean and the Magdalenian ..... p. 43
The first true Magdalénian ..... p. 43
The conquest of the underground world ..... p. 43
The lascaux sanctuary (Montignac) : the prehistoric Sistine Chapel ..... p. 44

4. THE MIDDLE MAGADALENIAN. FROM 16,000 TO 13,000 YEARS AGO (A. R.) ..... p. 49

The Cap Blanc ..... p. 50
Abri Reverdit ..... p. 53
Les Combarelles ..... p. 55
Font-de-Gaume ..... p. 57
Bernifal ..... p. 59
Rouffignac ..... p. 61

5. THE UPPER MAGADALENIAN. FROM 11,000 TO 9,500 YEARS AGO (A. R.) ..... p. 67

La Madeleine ..... p. 68
Villepin ..... p. 70
Laugerie-Basse ..... p. 70
Raymonden ..... p. 73
Rochereil ..... p. 77
Teyjat ..... p. 77
Limeuil ..... p. 81

6. THE MESOLITHIC AND NEOLITHIC. FROM 9,500 TO 3,000 B.C. (J.R.-L.) ..... p. 83

The Mesolithic and early Neolithic : from the woods to open clearings ..... p. 85
The Mesolithic culture : forest hunters ..... p. 85
The first step toward a farming culture ..... p. 86
The stone axe farmers ..... p. 86
The polished stone culture ..... p. 86
Middle Neolithic burials in caves and dolmens ..... p. 86
The chambered tombs : house of the dead or monument for the living ? ..... p. 91
Late Neolithic causewayed camps and collective cave burials ..... p. 92
Changes in the final Neolithic ..... p. 98

7. FROM THE DAWN OF COPPER TO THE IRON AGE : FROM 3,000 TO 700 B.C. (J.R.-L.) ..... p. 102

The rise of the Early Bronze Age and the first Perigord princes ..... p. 102
Prosperity in the Middle Bronze Age : weapons and ornaments ..... p. 107
A preview of the Final Bronze Age ..... p. 112
The heyday of the Perigord Bronze Age ..... p. 113
The end of the Bronze Age in the Perigord ..... p. 115
Towards new beginnings : the first Iron Age in the Perigord ..... p. 119
The real face in the Perigord ..... p. 120

CAVES, ROCK-SHELTERS, AND SITES : OPEN TO THE PUBLIC ..... p. 122

MUSEUMS ..... p. 123

MAPS ..... p. 124-125

BIBLIOGRAPHY ..... p. 126

In La Beune Valley at Masnaigre, to the left of an Upper Périgordian living site is a stained cliff withthe remains of building activity from recent history.

Front Cover :
Lascaux Cave.
Three red deer from the Frieze of the Deer.

Back Cover
The Bonarme Dolmen in Saint-Pardoux-et-Vielvic.
The Dolmen de Cayrelea, or Lou Ped de la Vache, is still half buried within an earthen mound andcovered with debris. One enters through the trapezoidal chamber by passing through the arch and asupport. The cap-stone is supported by two large parallel stones that form an entry corridor. This capstone bears two impressions which people generally see as of a cow's hoofprints.

 Ce livre a été imprimé par Pollina à Luçon - 85 - France. La photocomposition a été réalisée par ALFA-CSR à Bordeaux - 33. Mise en page du studio des Editions Sud-Ouest à Bordeaux. Photogravure de Photogravure System à Luçon - 85. La couverture a été tirée par l'Imprimerie Raynard à La Guerche de Bretagne - 35 et pelliculée par Pollina - 85. ISBN 2.87901.062.4 - Editeur : 234.01.05.06.92. N° d'impression : 15046